SOUL MATE AURAS

How Find Your Soul Mate & "Happily Ever After"

Embrosewyn Tazkuvel

Published by Kaleidoscope Productions
1467 Siskiyou Boulevard, #9; Ashland, OR 97520
www.kaleidoscope-publications.com
ISBN 978-0-938001-48-5

Cover design & book layout by Sumara Elan Love
www.3wizardz.com

OTHER CAPTIVATING, THOUGHT-PROVOKING BOOKS
by Embrosewyn Tazkuvel

WORDS OF POWER AND TRANSFORMATION
101+ Magickal Words and Sigils of Celestine Light to Manifest Your Desires

AURAS
How To See, Feel And Know

Secret Earth Series
INCEPTION *(Book 1)*
DESTINY *(Book 2)*

UNLEASH YOUR PSYCHIC POWERS

Psychic Awakening Series
CLAIRVOYANCE *(Book 1)*
TELEKINESIS *(Book 2)*
DREAMS *(Book 3)*

LOVE YOURSELF
Secret Key To Transforming Your Life

22 STEPS TO THE LIGHT OF YOUR SOUL

PSYCHIC SELF DEFENSE

ORACLES OF CELESTINE LIGHT
Complete Trilogy of Genesis, Nexus &Vivus

True love is extraordinary. Never take it for granted and it will never fail you. Love abundantly, with passion and tenderness and it will always be at your side. Walk hand and hand along eternity's path and true love will always light the way. Ever nurture and revere it and it shall continually enrich and uplift you beyond the celestial rainbow.

~22 Steps to the Light of Your Soul

TABLE OF CONTENTS

*Once in awhile, right in the middle of an ordinary life,
love gives us a fairy tale.*

~Unknown

Someday someone is going to look at you with a light in their eyes you've never seen. They'll look at you like you're everything they've been searching for their entire lives. Wait for it, its coming!

~Unknown

How do I love thee? Let me count the ways. I love thee to the depth and breadth and height my soul can reach.

~Elizabeth Barrett Browning

~♥~

INTRODUCTION

The romantic dream of finding your Soul Mate, the person with whom you resonate on every level of your being, is more than a wishful notion. It is a deeply embedded, primal desire that persists on some level despite what may have been years of quiet, inner frustration and included relationships that while fulfilling on some levels, still fell short of the completeness of a Soul Mate.

Once found, your relationship with your Soul Mate can almost seem like a dream at times. It will be all you expected and probably much more. Having never previously had a relationship that resonated in harmony and expansiveness on every level of your being, you will have had nothing to prepare you for its wonder. Having never stood atop a mountain that tall with an expansiveness so exhilarating, once experienced, a committed relationship with your Soul Mate will give you a bliss and fulfillment such as you probably only imagined in fairy tales.

Everything of course is not perfect. All relationships, even the very best and most harmonious, still have frictions and disagreements from time to time. But because of your harmonic resonance with one another, conflicts between you and your Soul Mate will tend to just be little bumps in the road, quickly passed with resumed harmony, not ever widening cracks and expanding pot holes of unhappiness and stagnation.

Having seen and strongly felt auric fields and energy center connections of people for the past six decades, I became fascinated with the energetic interplay between couples, especially after I finally found my own Soul Mate, and realized from personal experience how profound the personal growth and expansion can be between two people who are in harmonic resonance with all of their energy centers.

As you read through this book you will learn how to be drawn to and find your Soul Mate in this great big world. It may be the person down the street that you grew up with and have known all of your life but never recognized for who they truly are. Or, it may be a stranger, speaking a foreign tongue, and living in a country on the far side of the world.

The thrust of this book is learning how to recognize the auric field and energy connections of your Soul Mate. But it does not rely on your aura sensing abilities alone. Even if you never learn to see or feel auras, you will still be able to find your Soul Mate with additional search techniques and knowledge of highly successful and loving couples that are shared in detail. Even after you are seeing and feeling radiant auras, the additional tools and knowledge provided will help confirm what the aura and energy connections tell you.

I am so thrilled to have the opportunity to share the invaluable information and techniques in this book with you and other Soul Mate seekers in the world. Your Soul Mate is out there. And you *can* find them. Once discovered, it's up to you where you go from there. But I promise you that if you unite your lives together, you are going to embark on the ride of your life!

Namaste,

Embrosewyn Tazkuvel

~ ♥ ~

Chapter 1

I FOUND MY WIFE!

My Wedding Day : September 22, 1996

Soul Mate Auras

My whole life changed dramatically and forever on a comfortably warm summer's night, as I sat leaning back against a wall in a folding chair at the rear of a large conference room, along with my companion of nine years Skye, waiting along with about thirty other people for an informational meeting to begin. I was a forty year old, divorced father of three incredible children, two of which had recently moved back with me after having lived halfway around the world with their mother in France for the previous six years. Though my relationship with Skye was mostly as super compatible adventurers, I was happy in the relationship and didn't have a wandering eye for other women. But I did look at people's auras. It was a lifelong fascination of mine.

I was sitting on the left side edge of the center aisle. As the meeting was about to begin, two latecomers passed by and moved toward the front of the room, which was the only place remaining with vacant seats. Watching the two women from the rear as they walked forward I recognized Julia, an elderly lady I knew slightly. Walking beside her was a tall, slim woman with lovely, straight, wheat blonde hair falling to her waist.

She had already passed by before I took notice of her, so I had not seen her face. But I saw something else far, far more important. Something that literally almost made me topple over in my chair. Like sinuous, sizzling bolts of electricity I saw seven colored cords of auric energy leaping out of my body and connecting to the mysterious lady now sitting in the front row.

Seven! Seven energy connections! I was connecting, unspoken, with an unknown lady on all seven of our auric energy centers! My mouth gaped open in incredulous disbelief. I was in the room with my Soul Mate. It was unimaginable. But it was true, it was real. I didn't know what would happen next. She might be married with five kids in tow. But I knew I had to meet her. And I knew my life would never be the same.

Reveling in my astounding good fortune, I could barely contain my excitement waiting anxiously for the meeting to end so I could rush over and ask Julia to introduce me to her friend. Impatiently whiling away the tediously long minutes, I reflected on the mystique and wonder of Soul Mates and my own long journey to this fateful night.

Finding, loving and living happily ever after with your Soul Mate, the person you have a perfect resonance with, is a romantic yearning within the hearts of many people, both men and women. It is a deep, almost primal desire that may fade with years of falling short of the ideal with other relationships, as it had for me. But the unspoken ember of hope that it might someday, somehow manifest, never entirely disappears and is ever ready to erupt in wondrous flame should the magical moment unexpectedly arrive.

Most adults of any age, despite earlier disappointments, and even if they are currently in a committed relationship, would give serious attention to the man or woman they knew up front, beyond doubt, was the Soul Mate they had been hoping all of their life to someday meet. Being in their presence would be an irresistible force they could not deny. A meeting would have to occur. Whether a relationship blossomed between them after the first encounters, would depend upon the commitment to their current relationships with others, if any, plus their willingness to pursue a relationship that would certainly be different on many levels than any they had ever had before.

The reality of life is though many people remained married to the same person for their entire lives, most never find a perfect resonance or "happily ever after" with their Soul Mate. In fact, most people do not even recognize their Soul Mate when they encounter them, even if it is someone they have known and been friends with for years. How can this be? How can something so desired by so many people, be found and fulfilled by so few? Unfortunately, when seeking to find their Soul Mate, most people are looking for the wrong indicators, or they are currently incapable of recognizing the right ones.

I speak from personal experience of failure. Though I have seen and felt auras strongly for all of my life, it did not even occur to me when I married my first wife, a sweet and lovely French woman, that I should first check out our auric connections to see how compatible we were in other areas beyond our common religion and my spellbound attraction for her Frenchness and her delightfully charming accent. I never tired of hearing her speak!

My second long-term companion was an adventurous, free-spirited woman named Skye, whom I am still dear friends with, and whom I sat next to on that fateful night, waiting for the informational meeting to begin. When Skye and I first met, I had just gone through a wrenchingly painful divorce and was still trying to come to grips with the reality that I would probably never see my three children again, as they had gone to France with their mother, except for fleeting moments of joyous reunion followed shortly thereafter by another crushing separation. I vowed to never marry again. My utter first failure weighed upon me heavily. Nor could I conceive of a capacity to love anyone more than I had loved my first wife.

After divorce from her first husband some years earlier, Skye had the same sentiment. She had no children to encumber her from her previous relationship. Nor for medical reasons could she have any. That suited me as well, as I missed my children dearly and at that point in my life did not want any others to take their place.

With Skye, I was a little wiser than with my first wife. She was easy on the eyes, fun and up for any adventure, incredibly easy to get along with, didn't want an official marriage, couldn't have kids, and was content if our relationship was more about shared adventure and not so much about romance or intimacy. Plus, she loved quartz crystals, which was also a life-long love of mine. Those were many great points to begin laying a firm foundation for a long-term relationship. But this time around, I also looked at our auric connections. I felt them as well, intentionally probing, wanting to insure we were more compatible on energetic levels and had more in common than I had with my ex-wife.

There are seven major energy centers in the body. Each one swirls and spins a specific type of energy that tremendously affects your body, influencing everything from your thoughts and feelings to your fears, lusts, self-confidence and virtually every aspect of your being. In the Hindu world they are called Chakras. In the Celestine Light teachings that I use, they are called Root Ki's.

Harmony within the energy spheres between two people in a relationship is immensely helpful to creating a lasting, loving rapport. Absence of energetic connections dooms a relationship to frequent turmoil, or boring indifference and virtually separate lives, even though the couple may continue to remain married. For instance, if one person had a very empathetic energy center of the heart, but their mate was very cold and heartless, there would always be friction between them in that area. The more energy centers with disharmony, the more occasions will be present for contention and clashes to occur.

Contrarily, if they were both expressive of love, and empathetic and equally affected by the misfortune of other people or animals, their heart energy centers would have a sweet resonance with each other. A strong harmonious heart connection would lead to similar interests in entertainment, common ideals to create a happy home, raise children and mutually satisfying expressions of love and affection every day. The greater number of the seven energy centers that are in harmonic reverberation with one another, the more likely a relationship will last for the long term.

Most couples only have one to four energy centers in harmony. When five to six are in harmony they become Twin Flames. In your life you can discover several Twin Flames, of either sex, and the relationships do not need to be romantic or sexual.

Soul Mates have all seven of the primary energy centers in harmony and a Soul Mate is very extraordinary. Many people live their entire life and never encounter their fully harmonic soul companion. However, being Soul Mates does not imply that they are mirror clones of each other or will always have the same opinion about things. Nor that they will not still have disagreements and upsets between them from time to time. But when negative energy does arise between them will likely never escalate too greatly and will soon be dissipated by the love, mutual respect and abundant energy bonds they share.

The more energy centers in harmony the more likely couples will tend to like the same type of activities, have similar introverted or extroverted personalities, and simply be extremely comfortable with one another, never tiring of each other's company. Looking at the energy connections between me and Skye gave me confidence there was great potential in our relationship. We were not Soul Mates, but we had strong connections on four of our energy centers, and good connections on two others, so I knew she was a Twin Flame. Add in physical attraction and our common interests and I was confident we would get along well and be fulfilled over an extended period of time.

Nine years later, still enjoying each other's companionship and continuing to be fulfilled in the areas of our auric harmony, proved the strength of our energetic connections. We had fun together all across America and every week was a lively adventure, all in harmony and with great compatibility. Though neither of us was looking for a new partner and were both very satisfied in our relationship, we also knew and accepted that someday a Soul Mate might come into one of our lives and that would mean a change in our relationship. Sitting in the back of the room together that night, waiting for the meeting to begin, that fateful moment transpired.

Still counting the minutes for the interminably long meeting to be over, I realized I probably would not have recognized the significance of my Soul Mate if I had met her when I was younger. In my early years I had actually never heard of the concept of a Soul Mate and I was still learning the intricacies of auras. Though seven energies connections to another person would have been something to note, with my limited experience I couldn't be sure I wouldn't encounter another ten people like that the next day. In the meantime my hormones probably would have been directing my attention more to a girl I connected to only on the Vm.

The good news is, regardless of your age, despite any past disappointments you may have had, you can successfully locate, identify and verify your Soul Mate, anywhere they are in this great big world. It is not instantaneous. It will likely require patience and take time for you to be drawn together over the oftentimes vast distance that initially separates you. You'll need to learn some special techniques using auras that anyone can master if they are willing to practice. And it helps immensely if you are actually in a place in your life that you are happy with yourself, and are truly *ready* to meet your Soul Mate. I did it and I know you can too!

I Never Would Have Found My Soul Mate Without My Children

My nine years with Skye up to the moment of the meeting that night, had been fairly carefree. For the first few years neither of us had children living with us, or any other responsibilities tying us to any particular location. We both had independent businesses that allowed us to work anywhere in the world as long as we didn't mind doing it on a shoestring budget. After three years together, we decided to pool all of our pennies and buy a dilapidated 48 foot ferrocement sailboat in Florida to live aboard and rebuild over a couple of years, then cruise the world. But our project was permanently interrupted one miraculous summer, when after six years apart, my ex-wife in France agreed to let my two oldest children come for a two month visit and stay with Skye and I on our sailboat.

It was a glorious two months full of memories. But a big prickly issue came up just a day or two before it was time for my children to return to France. They refused to go back! I never spoke a word, or even hinted about such a scenario to either of them, so was as shocked as anyone when they made their united stand. Without going into detail, you can imagine this did not go over well with my ex-wife.

Soul Mate Auras

Our big sailboat suddenly became much too small for two adults and two energetic young teenagers, plus a parrot, to be living on full-time, so without any regrets and looking forward to a new adventure, we sold the boat and moved to land. After a year of living in the wilds of Florida, we decided we needed to find the most suitable location to give the kids one high school to attend 9th through 12th grade. We made a list of desirable locales based upon a long list of criteria including quality of the schools, climate, proximity to the ocean, crime rates, etc., In early June, we began an epic journey across the US in a two-vehicle camping caravan to personally investigate each city to see how we "felt" about it. We planned to return and settle in the one that by consensus felt most right.

"Feeling right" is where auras begin coming into play, even for people who do not realize it. Even for those who might be complete disbelievers in auras. We already knew the pros and cons of each town from our research before we visited it. If our choice was based purely on logic we would have just chosen the place that scored the highest on our initial grading and driven straight there. Well maybe not, because we wanted to use the opportunity to take a family vacation and let the kids experience some of the vastness and wonder of the USA. But you get the point I'm sure.

Scouting towns to relocate to is a wonderful example of the "feeling" power of auras and energy fields. On a smaller scale, looking for a house to buy and call a home engenders similar feelings once you find the right one.

Everything in and surrounding a town puts out a discernible and palpable bioenergy. The multiple energies interact with the auric field surrounding your body creating a feeling that stirs warm fuzzies inside of you if its right, and leaves you cold and disinterested if it's wrong. Though you may be able to pick out certain aspects that you liked, such as the town's architecture, or its parks, or the friendliness of the people, the final judgment will conclude with a feeling that sums all the energies from tangible to intangible that touched your aura. Anyone on a traveling search like ours to find the perfect place, in the end after noting the tangible reasons, would probably conclude like we all did, that it "just felt right."

We had narrowed our original list of twenty-two towns down to six before we began the migration. Our remaining candidates in order of our travel were: Pensacola, Florida; Fayetteville, Arkansas; Albuquerque/Taos, New Mexico; Sedona, Arizona; Ashland, Oregon; and Port Torwnsend, Washington. I had already been to all of those towns at some time in my past travels and knew I liked every one of them.

The first four all had alluring aspects, in addition to the quaint towns themselves: Pensacola, had miles and miles of astounding white sand beaches and a warm ocean to swim in; Fayetteville, the enchanting four seasons of the rounded mountain hills; Albuquerque with its picturesque Southwest pueblo architecture and super sunny climate; Taos the artists heaven, and luscious hot springs in the nearby mountains; Sedona with stunningly scenic red buttes and natural towers along with deliciously potent energy vortexes that entice visitors from all over the world.

A few weeks and many miles later, we crested Siskiyou Pass on the California-Oregon border. At 4300 feet above sea level, it is the highest point on the Interstate 5 freeway. Rounding big curve after big curve on the long, steep decline down from the pass, we were headed to Ashland, a city of 20,000 residents at the 2000 foot level and the picturesque guardian of the southern end of the forty-five mile long mountain-locked Rogue Valley. The delicious, "this is home" feeling hit all of us before we ever saw the infamous Shakespeare festival town. Descending from the pass, we marveled at 800 acre Emigrant Lake far below to the right, standing out like an enticing jewel. As we got closer to the southern end of the picturesque Rogue Valley, we noted with some amazement the startling contrast between the dry, sparsely vegetated east side and the green, profusely vegetated west side, with not even a mile separating the two starkly contrasting climate zones.

By the time we took the first exit and pulled into the nearby parking lot of the Albertson's supermarket, Skye was already telling us that exquisite tingling sensations were running up and down her body. Though less dramatic, all of us were also feeling strange and wonderful sensations as we first arrived in Ashland. There was nothing special about our first stop. It looked like a thousand other supermarket parking lots, with its generic adjacent businesses from the drugstore to the laundromat. Nevertheless, even though we still had not seen the quaint downtown, the renown Lithia Park, the historic neighborhoods, or checked out the high school, the feeling, the aura, the "force" of Ashland, resonated within each one of us. Before we ever left the Albertson's parking lot, we all knew we had found our new home and there would be no point at all in continuing on to check out Sequim, Washington.

The First Meeting

Still waiting for the arduously, long meeting to be over so I could go introduce myself to the lady I had waited all of my adult life for, I reflected that I would need to give my children a heart-felt thanks. If they had not come back to live with me and aborted my cruise around the world, I would not have been in Ashland at that moment in time, with my Soul Mate sitting a mere twenty feet away and destiny about to finally call at a time I could actually answer.

I naively assumed if meeting my Soul Mate was destiny, then it would happen regardless of where I was living at the time and fairly early in my life, so we could have a long life together. Surely we would be irresistibly drawn together like magnets, right? But at that moment, with forty years behind me, including one divorce and three wonderful children, I felt I had failed as a father by not being in their lives every day, and a second long-term relationship that while wonderfully harmonious, was not at a Soul Mate level, I was more inclined to unabashedly seize the opportunity and less inclined to give destiny any more leeway.

After the meeting Skye went off to chat with some of her friends and I hurried over to intercept Julia before she and my mystery Soul Mate escaped the room as they were already heading for an exit near the front.

I quickly caught up to them and greeted them with a friendly, "Hi Julia," followed shortly by, "Who's your friend?"

As I waited for Julia to answer, I looked for the first time at the flawless face and into the big, piecing blue eyes of my mystery Soul Mate. I had to make a conscious effort to keep my mouth from gaping open in wonder. She was radiant! In my eyes, she was the most beautiful woman I had ever met.

Julia gave a slight all-knowing smile as she noticed my blatant staring at her friend. "This is Sumara," she introduced.

Wow! Her name was as exotic and entrancing as her beauty and the astounding vibrant bands of energy that were coursing between us.

I talked with the two of them for another five minutes. Without any disrespect for Julia I don't remember a word she said. Though I might have politely nodded and murmured acknowledgment, the truth was all of my attention was riveted on Sumara.

Unfortunately, I couldn't think of any additional conversation to engage them in that would keep them there for even a few minutes longer, or any reason I could come up with that we should meet again. Luckily, Julia introduced the opening.

"Some of us will be getting together at Sumara's house tomorrow to talk about marketing the products we were introduced to at this meeting. As you have some marketing expertise why don't you come and share some of your knowledge with us?"

"Yes, of course. I can't think of any place I'd rather be," I agreed with relief. Then with a smile, a wave and a cheery goodbye, Sumara and Julia walked out the door and I began counting the minutes to the appointed time for my hopefully fateful rendezvous the next day.

Traveling back home in the car with Skye, though I really knew nothing about Sumara yet or her current life situation, or availability in starting a relationship, I knew I had to at least mention meeting her to Skye. Any normal woman would have their jealous radar up and probably would have freaked out as soon as they sensed my interest in another woman. But Skye was special and our relationship was not a typical one. Not only was she very knowledgeable about the effects of auric energy on human relations, but she was in better control of her emotions than anyone I had ever met. She reasoned with her mind as well as felt with her heart. This trait enabled her to never get too high or too low in any situation.

Nevertheless, she completely surprised me with her reaction.

"While you were talking with your friends after the meeting," I began hesitantly, "I met someone you need to know about."

"Who?" Skye asked with innocent curiosity.

I gulped, took a deep breath and exhaled slowly, "a lady I had a lot of energy connections with," I spoke quietly.

"Who?" Skye wondered. "Was it someone I met?"

"No, I met her after the meeting when you were off talking to some other people," I explained.

"She was the lady with the waist length long blonde hair that came to the meeting with Julia," I elaborated.

"What is her name?" Skye asked still trying to place who I was talking about.

"Sumara," I said simply. "I didn't learn her last name. I only talked to her briefly."

"Sumara," Skye repeated slowly as if in deep reflection. "Her name is familiar."

"Do you know her?" I asked surprised and curious.

"I'm sure I've never met her," Skye elaborated, "but her name somehow resonates in my heart. I know I want to meet her."

Well that was a pleasantly unexpected reaction!

"I'm going to a marketing meeting with Julia and some other people at Sumara's house tomorrow," I explained. "I'll find out more about her then and let you know if it turns out she is as special as she seems she might be."

"To both of us," I added.

Arriving at the meeting the following day, I had eyes only for Sumara. Our energy connection was potent. It was like an ambrosia to me. I was filled with exquisite euphoria and happiness just being in the same room with her, even if she was on the opposite side talking to someone else.

I did make a memorable impression on Sumara that day, but not necessarily completely favorable. Her house was tastefully decorated and had several one-of-a-kind works of art. As I was standing in front of her bookcase in animated explanation about something, I knocked a unique layered vase flying with a flourish of my hand. With a resounding crash it hit the floor and broke off all of the layers! Beet red with embarrassment, I was sure I had just ruined any chance I had to start a relationship with Sumara, before it even had the opportunity to begin.

Thankfully, Sumara did not scream in despair at the loss of one of her prized possessions. To my great relief, as I squatted crestfallen with embarrassment to pick up the broken pieces, she came over to help me. Forgivingly holding my eyes with her gaze she told me sweetly not to worry about it. She held up the broken vase. The thick vase portion was still intact. It was only the fragile flowing layers at the top that had broken off.

"I think it still looks good as a simply flower vase," she said with a radiant smile in my direction. "I'm going to keep it. And I'll remember you with a little humor every time I see it."

Soul Mate Auras

I was so relieved I hadn't blown my chance to get to know her better. Sumara told me later, after we were in a relationship, that she had thought I was a little weird from the beginning, in a cute sort of way. So she just chalked it up to part of my endearing eccentricity.

Immediately after the get-together I was in the same quandary as after the meeting the previous night. What reason could I come up with to justify our continued relationship, as simple as it was? During our conversation Sumara mentioned she had just connected to the Internet for the very first time (1995) the day before and was still trying to figure out how to use email and other features. It was my 'ah-ha' moment. I offered to send her an email when I got home and it was the first task I did as soon as I arrived back at my house near Emigrant Lake. I had the honor of sending her the very first email she ever received!

For the next week we corresponded by email many times during the day and night. We learned of several common interests, especially building and living in close-knit communities. She had lived for seven years in a Native American community and I was the visionary of the Celestopea Project to create an independent, self-sufficient community floating on the sea.

Still looking for ways to connect with her personally, I offered in an email to come over and give her some more marketing tips to help her with her business. She agreed that would be nice and I was knocking on her door later that afternoon. After helping her with a few things, I invited her to go with me on a walk up in the mountains above town as it was a warm, beautiful fall day. As we walked through the woods I felt like a schoolboy with his first crush. I had never felt such powerful feelings of love, of belonging, of oneness, as I did with Sumara.

Tentatively, to give her the option of yea or nay, I asked her if it would be alright if I held her hand. Yes, I was a little strange. In response, she put her hand in mine and I was suddenly transported to heaven on earth. Auras are very powerful. I can sense a person's mood and even the type of thoughts they are thinking from the other side of a big room. But to actually touch someone is to receive an abundance of auric energy that can sometimes almost overwhelm me with emotions and understanding about that person and their current life challenges. Holding hands with Sumara was all that multiplied by a hundred. Presiding over all other energies was the profound realization that this was my Soul Mate, the woman I had searched for all of my life and almost given up hope of ever finding. I knew at that very moment, despite any and all the obstacles, she would become my wife and eternal mate.

More surprisingly, I knew that day that we would have a child together in the future. A true love child. I had long ago sworn off ever having children again. And considering our ages and the current challenging status of both our lives, such an outcome seemed very improbable. Yet I knew it was true. Just as I knew that no matter what obstacles were thrown before us, we would be together from that moment on. And there was no person, or force on earth or in the universe that would be able to prevent our union.

Almost exactly one year later, on September 22, 1996, we were married, up in the mountains, surrounded by friends and family, under an arching bower of flowers, next to a gurgling creek, on a glorious, sunny day. Skye was Sumara's Maid of Honor.

In July of 1998, Sumara gave birth to our amazing daughter, Angeline; a true indigo Child of Light and an inspiration and sunbeam of joy to all who are blessed to know her.

After I returned home late that night from my time on the mountain when I first held Sumara's hand, I woke Skye to tell her what I discovered.

"Skye. I have some important news," I whispered, gently touching her shoulder to awaken her.

She was wide awake right away. "Remember how we have always kept open the possibility that one of us might one day find our Soul Mate?" I reminded Skye quietly. She nodded her head slowly and I could see in the immediate darkening of her aura that she suspected what I was going to say next. And the first impact of that thought on her did not engender feelings of joy.

I took a deep breath and slowly exhaled as I reached out and held Skye's hand in mine.

"Sumara is my Soul Mate," I said simply. "She is the one I have waited for and always hoped to someday find. We connect harmoniously on all of our energy centers."

Skye began to cry a bit, which was very unlike her. I was at a complete loss at what I could say or do to comfort her, but I tried.

"I don't want you to be hurt Skye. I love you and appreciate you so much." I spoke tenderly with great affection.

"I don't want our time together to stop. I have no desire for us to end our relationship. I have no idea how this will work out. But this is a force of the aura, of my very being and essence that is impossible to resist."

To my surprise, Skye's aura began to change. The darkening that had happened was quickly replaced by a lightening. The colors became more vibrant, sending out many jewels of light. I sensed her tears of sadness were now mixed with joy. I didn't know what to make of such an energetic combination.

Her first words in reply explained everything. "I welcome her to our family." Though I had always known it, that moment it became so abundantly clear that I was in the presence of a remarkable woman!

It was my turn to be shocked, and I was! Sitting on the bed, Skye held both my hands and explained as she wiped away her tears.

"Since you first said her name, I have known her, even though I have yet to meet her in person. Each day, as you have talked about her, I have felt connected to her stronger and stronger in so many ways. You have been sad thinking that by getting together with Sumara, you were going to need to end our relationship. I don't think that is true, although our relationship will probably change and there is still a part of me that is sad about that part of it. But Sumara is your Soul Mate and I know that is a force you cannot turn away from. I'm sure she is also my Twin Flame, my sister of light. We may not connect on all of our energy centers as you two do, but surely we connect on many of them."

"Don't worry," she consoled me holding my hand in hers. "I am very anxious to meet her and I'm sure it will all work out."

I was somewhat dumbfounded by Skye's reaction. Would Sumara feel the same way about Skye? And how would that all work? It was an unexplored, unknown, unfathomable, relationship dynamic.

Sumara and Skye soon did meet, and they immediately became the sisters neither of them had from their parents.

Skye's first words of greeting to Sumara were the same as her acceptance of her to me the night before, "welcome to the family."

Over the nearly twenty years since, the three of us have shared many adventures together as well as many dreams and actions for the future. Skye is still open to finding the bliss of her Soul Mate. But until then, and hopefully still after then, with a +1, the three of us continue to forge a unique and fulfilling life together.

IN ALL THE WORLD, THERE IS NO HEART
FOR ME LIKE YOURS. IN ALL THE WORLD,
THERE IS NO LOVE FOR YOU LIKE MINE.

MAYA ANGELOU

Falling in love is easy. But staying in love is very special.

~Unknown

Chapter 2

CATALYST FOR EVOLVING

This story would not be complete without an epilogue to what happened to me afterward and to Sumara and Skye in different ways as well. One of the hallmarks of entering a new Soul Mate or Twin Flame relationship is all of your energy centers are greatly stimulated because of the harmonic interaction with another person so in tune with your essence. The harmonic stimulation causes your energy centers to rapidly expand. For months and maybe years afterward, as long as your relationship still has a blossom of love, your energy centers stay expanded beyond the level they were formerly.

The expansion of your energy centers when you begin sharing a life with your Soul Mate or Twin Flame will be a very exciting and fulfilling time for you personally. There will be a renewed excitement and enthusiasm for all aspects of your life, including many that may have been languishing. If you are an artist of any specialty from music, to art, to performance, you will likely be motivated with excitement to create new and inspired art. If you have always wanted to start a business, but have been a bit too afraid to actually do it, you may suddenly find the courage and fortitude to begin. If you have had relationship challenges with friends or family you will likely be motivated to give renewed and extra effort to resolve them. Getting together with your Soul Mate or Twin Flame can almost seem like the wave of a magical, transformational wand. Like a butterfly emerging from a cocoon, a glorious new you that has always been there inside suddenly bursts out!

All three of us experienced tremendous personal growth and expansion in many areas of our lives. Uniting together proved to be a powerful catalyst for change and improvement. Old thought patterns that had proved valueless and even detrimental in some cases, were cast aside and we became open to receiving greater enlightenment.

For me personally, I experienced a meteoric rise in my psychic abilities that would have been almost unbelievable if Skye and Sumara hadn't been present to witness the metamorphosis. That alone was an abiding testimony for me of the rightness and harmony of my connection with Sumara and power of three in our union with Skye.

Soul Mate Auras

I had seen auras from my infancy. I knew it was simply a function of how I focused my eyes, so I accepted them as normal for me, even though they might be derided by others. But when it came to virtually every other psychic ability, it was me that was the derider. Some years earlier Skye convinced me to go with her to see a well-known psychic in Seattle named Evelyn Jenkins. She channeled in higher beings to impart words of wisdom to people. At the time, coming from a science background in school which I had completely aligned with, I was of the opinion that anyone who believed in channeling had marbles for brains and I wasn't hesitant to let naive, misguided people know my opinions. I was certain that belief in psychic abilities beyond seeing auras, insinuated at least a few screws loose upstairs. Skye on the other hand was a big believer in the paranormal.

We had two meetings with Ms. Jenkins. The first was a disaster because of my overt skepticism and Evelyn was so disturbed by my attitude that she said she never wanted to see me again. During the following week, I became obsessed with the need to go to another session with Evelyn, only this time with an open heart and mind. Reluctantly, she agreed.

I came to see her the second time with more humility and the results were beyond any of our expectations. I saw and heard amazing phenomenon, including a massive blue beam of scintillating energy blasting from me to Evelyn, then to Skye and back to me. Evelyn who had been a professional channel for over ten years was so dumbfounded by what she had also seen and heard that she said the purpose of her channeling had been fulfilled and she never needed to channel again. Initially, it was very difficult for me to suspend my disbelief at what occurred, what I saw and felt. But before I left that night, I knew I could not deny it, even though much to the dismay of my scientific brain, I could not explain it.

Some years passed and though I was more open than previously to the validity of paranormal possibilities, I still didn't give it much thought. And I still considered most believers to be very naïve. And that's putting it nicely. I had no inkling about how greatly my life was about to change.

When Sumara and I first got together, she and I both knew Skye had to remain a very close part of our lives. Skye felt exactly the same. She couldn't conceive of not being in a close, daily relationship with me and Sumara. But exactly what kind of relationship was that going to be? None of us knew. We were all open to exploring new relationship possibilities but weren't quite sure how to go about it. After three months, talking endlessly among ourselves and even seeking counseling with multiple experts from a psychologist to a channeler, we were no closer to a solution. No relationship arrangement felt right.

Honestly, I was at my wits end. Trying to figure out the correct relationship dynamic that was respectful and beneficial to all three of us, and kept all of us in each other's lives, had left me frustrated and almost without hope of finding a solution. I was sitting alone at my desk at home around 2:00 AM on a night in late December 1995, which I later discovered was the exact moment of the winter solstice.

Skye was asleep in another room and Sumara was in Puerto Rico attending the wedding of one of her brothers. Thinking there was one last thing I could try, even if it seemed almost ludicrous to me, I called out loud, "If there are any higher beings up there that have a solution to my problem, now is the time to make yourself known and help me out."

Immediately words involuntarily came out of my mouth that I did not speak, even though it was my voice and I was perfectly conscious and aware that I was speaking. "I am Arnosassium. I can help you."

I looked around furtively to the right and left. Did those words really come out of my mouth? Just in case this was somehow real, I grabbed my little mini tape recorder and pushed 'record.' Then though I felt somewhat foolish, I asked another question aloud. "Who are you Arnosassium?"

Once again my mouth just started involuntarily talking. I'm not sure I could have stopped it even if I wanted to. The voice was my voice, and I was fully conscious of everything being said. A big part of me at that point thought I was just answering my own questions and somehow pretending to be someone wiser in the answer. But Arnosassium began to tell me things I had never conceived. He told me he was one of 397 Galactic Energy Beings that formed the Celestine Order of Light (COOL). Some were male, some female, and each had a specialty, which could be called upon to help those in need.

"Something like angels?" I wondered.

"Something like that," Arnosassium agreed.

(A big part of me still thought I was just talking to myself at this point.)

He explained his specialty was to help people who were channeling higher beings for the very first time, because his energy was very harmonious and easy to receive.

Then something very odd began to happen. With each new answer that came from Arnosassium in response to my audible questions, my responding voice began to change. An accent began to manifest that became stronger and more pronounced with each answer. Additionally, the stronger Arnosassium's strange accent became the more my consciousness and awareness of the questions and answers began to fade. Thankfully the recorder was still recording or I would have had no way of knowing the final answers. The questions were still in my normal voice. But the answers were definitely alien in tone and accent.

Arnosassium told me that I would be the channel for all 397 Galactics of the Celestine Order of Light, both male and female, and that each would have their own personality, voice and accent. He instructed me to begin the very next day by inviting Philos, whose specialty was Celestine Vibronics healing and who could answer my relationship questions. Apparently, though I had no memory of it, Philos and I had many connections previous to life in this physical body.

Most importantly, Arnosassium gave us the long sought after answer about what would be the most harmonious state for our three-way relationship; one that would be fulfilling and expansive for all and maintain the unity of the power of three, while still allowing Sumara and I to bask in our Soul Mate relationship and leave Skye available to find hers at some point in the future.

By the time it was over, I felt like I was awakening from a deep sleep. After I was fully into conscious awareness, I rushed out of the room to share my amazing experience with Skye. At first, knowing my prankster nature and skepticism and even ridicule of people who believed in channeling, she thought I was playing a joke on her. Even when she realized I was serious she had a hard time believing it, as after all it was me, the great skeptic.

The following day we drove to a remote spot overlooking a large lake outside of town. Skye had a set of test questions she was prepared to ask if I successfully brought in another being through channel. I closed my eyes and called out in my mind for Arnosassium. In moments he was quickly present as he had been the night before.

Skye turned on the tape recorder and started to ask her questions. Though the first couple of answers were in my own voice, Arnosassium's unique accent was quickly present. Soon Arnosassium introduced Philos, and as Philos came in Arnosassium bid us goodbye and faded away. Philos had a very heavy, almost Scottish accent that was quite different from Arnosassium's more high pitched lilting way of speaking.

Very quickly as Philos began to answer Skye's questions, my conscious awareness began to fade. It was obviously much easier to get into a trance when I didn't have to also ask the questions! Over an hour and many dozens of questions and answers later, I awoke from my trance. I had no memory of anything that had been asked or answered and needed to go home and listen to the recording to be as astounded as Skye already was from having witnessed and experienced it. I heard her cry on the tape, but it was tears of joy and happiness at what was being revealed by Philos, And also a powerful tugging in her heart as she too realized that she was reconnecting to a cherished, long, lost friend.

We Express Mailed a copy of the recordings of both Arnosassium and Philos to Sumara in Puerto Rico and she was just as enthralled and couldn't wait to get back home so she could be present for the next channeling. And what a long line of *next* it ended up being. Apparently, there had never been a channel on this Earth for the 397 Galactics of COOL. Individuals, if they had a limited ability, could communicate with them one on one as needed for their specialty. But there had never been one person who could channel them all. They were like kids in a candy store! They all wanted to be channeled and be able to speak and help.

For the next two months, Sumara, Skye and I would spend many hours each day channeling different beings. Many Galactics had their chance to come into a full body, full trance channel for the first time on this Earth and share their wisdom. In each case, I had no memory of what transpired and would need to listen to the tape to learn about the session. Sadly, channeling soon became so common and was taking so many hours each day that we stopped recording most sessions. Skye and Sumara just took notes of important points and shared them with me, but over the years many have been lost.

Some of the Galactic energies were not as easy for my body to handle as Philos' and Arnosassium's. Female energies were always more of a challenge. My masculine vocal chords were not well-suited to project their softer feminine voices. And some of the Galactics simply had very alien energy. They were not human and my human energy had sometimes considerable convolutions meshing with theirs. I would lay prone on a bed while channeling and Sumara and Skye related how my body would buck and thrash about so much when bringing in alien energies that often times I would have fallen off the bed if they hadn't caught me and pushed me back!

As it turns out, many of the Galactics had personal connections to people on Earth; sometimes very personal. Many of these connected people began to find their way to me, sometimes from all the way across the country. They would have the opportunity while I was in a trance channel, to meet and talk with their personal Galactic. Sumara or Skye were most often present as witnesses and said the meetings were often full of overwhelming recognition, love, happiness and many tears of joy, especially when the Galactic shared a moment of recall from their past together that the people remembered.

Despite pleas to continue, I decided to stop channeling Galactics who were connected to other people. Though I felt very good about helping people reconnect with someone so important in their life, because I was not consciously present during channelings I felt I was simply losing too many hours of my own life during the void.

Before such time however, Philos asked if we could hold weekly sessions open to the general public where he would first deliver a talk on a subject he felt was important, followed by an open question and answer session where people could ask questions about anything they desired. We did this for one year and it became quite popular and we would have a large room packed with people each week. After the year was up, Philos said he was done speaking to the public as he had already imparted all the wisdom people needed to lead expansive, healthy, balanced lives, and it was now up to us and them, to begin living what we had learned.

Being able to manifest the blessing of full body, full trance channeling of 397 different beings was more than my greatest expectation of psychic ability. But it was one of only several psychic and paranormal abilities and powers that I began to exhibit once the catalyst of my union with Sumara had occurred. And it was further amplified by the power of three that was created as Skye remained an active part of our lives and the three of us worked in unison on projects of importance.

Today, I am fairly well-known in the psychic and paranormal worlds and have several popular books published including, *Auras: How to See, Feel & Know*, *Psychic Self Defense*, *Unleash Your Psychic Powers*, *Telekinesis*, *Clairvoyance* and *Dreams*. None of these books would have ever been written and few of my paranormal adventures other than with auras, ever experienced, if not for the catalyst of expansion that started on a warm fall day, on a picturesque mountain overlooking a beautiful valley, at the magical moment when I first held Sumara's hand. My whole world, my life, my hopes, dreams and aspirations, all changed on that fateful day. And I'm so glad and fulfilled that they did.

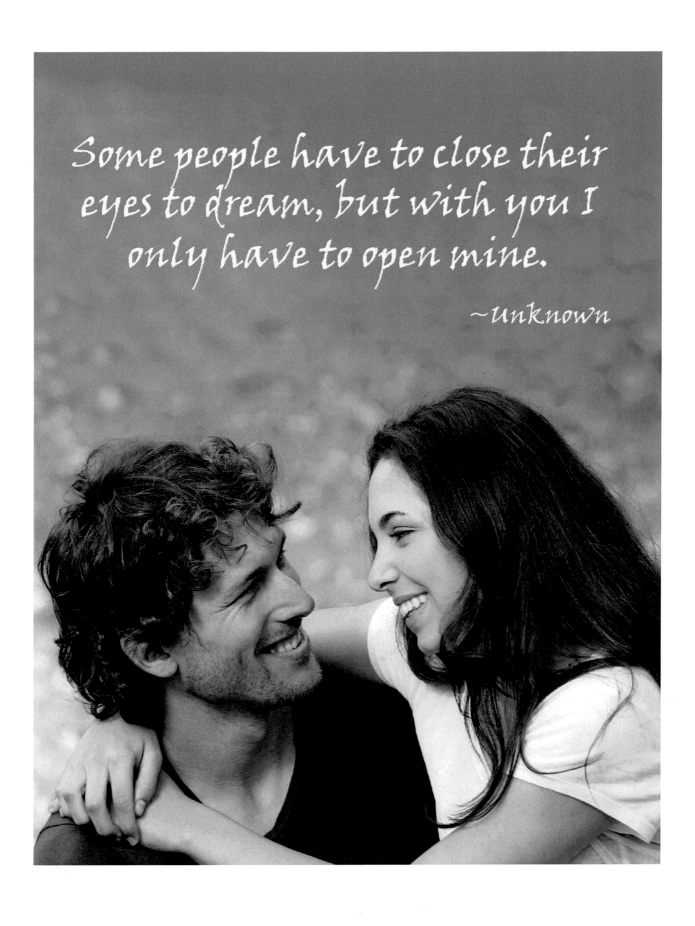

Ask nothing of love but to have it willingly reciprocated. The harmonic reverberation that occurs with reciprocated love will transform you. It will uplift you. It will make you more than you ever could aspire to otherwise. You will be blessed with a singular warmth that rhythmically stirs your luminous soul as love flows in and love flows out.

22 Steps to the Light of Your Soul

Chapter 3

THE SEVEN ENERGY CENTERS OF THE BODY

As the energy centers of the human body play a pivotal role in every person's auric field and an equally essential role in the energy between couples, we need to take a moment to elaborate on what they are, how they work, and why their vitality and influence are so important.

What Are the Energy Centers of the Body?

Several faiths and philosophies from as far back as 600 AD and ranging from Hinduism to Kaballah, have had detailed teachings about the energy centers and auric fields of the human body. In most traditions there are seven energy centers that correspond to organs and areas of influence in the body.

Faith healing, especially involving the 'laying on of hands' and the ancient Chinese practice of Qigong, have been around since the dawn of recorded history. In more modern times, specific methods of energy healing such as Reiki have been developed and gained attention. In Fengrun, China, until it was closed for political reasons in 2001, there was an entire modern hospital and a community of 4,000 people, that centered its healing work around the ancient bioenergy techniques of Qigong. All of these methods of healing have proven effective with often-times miraculous results, even though for the longest time there was no scientific means to account for it.

The perception of energy healing and the reality of the human aura have been validated and verified by recent breakthroughs in scientific measuring equipment, particularly the SQUID Magnetometer, which can be calibrated to detect even minute biomagnetic fields put out by the human body. The same fields and centers of energy that sensitive people and faith healers have described for millenia are now being accepted as reality by some members of the traditional health community because of the ability to objectively measure the bio fields of energy.

How Do the Body Energy Centers Work?

Many ancient societies have traditions acknowledging the human auric field. The Chinese call it the Chi force (pronounced kee). In Hindu tradition it is 'prana,' the life force that permeates all creation.

Chinese acupuncture has been used to tap into the natural energy flow of the body for pain relief and to alleviate some forms of human sickness and malaise for thousands of years. Acupuncture is based upon the principle of thin lines of energy running through the body from the bottoms of the feet to the top of the head. These lines are called 'meridians' and they pass through every organ and part of the body carrying the life force of energy. Tapping into one of the meridians at a convenient point with a needle stuck shallowly into the body allows the stimulus to affect every organ and point along the entire length of that particular meridian through the length of the body.

One of my elderly aunts visited one of the first acupuncture centers on the East Coast back in the 1960's for pain relief. After her initial very successful pain treatment the acupuncturist asked her if she had any other problems he might help. She casually mentioned she had become deaf in her right ear some years ago and wondered almost jokingly, whether acupuncture could be of any benefit.

With all seriousness the acupuncturist said he felt it might and stuck a single small needle in just below her ear. When she returned home, she couldn't stop talking with well-founded excitement about her acupuncture miracle. She related how she had instantly heard a loud pop after the needle was inserted and her hearing was suddenly completely restored!

Celestine Vibronics goes into even more detail than acupuncture, showing the flow of energy through the body as it travels through three pairs of key entry and exit points called Alpha/Omega gateways. The flow of energy as seen in the diagram is up one side of the body and down the other. Because of this, it creates counter currents that initiate and maintain the omnidirectional movement of the spherical energy centers in the body.

Though I am fascinated by the underlying scientific principles that explain the human energy flow and auric field, my deep understanding of their presence and function comes from the simple fact that I have been seeing and feeling them for 60 years! I have spent countless hours on innumerable days, in every conceivable setting, observing the human aura on people young and old, healthy and ill. I have been with babies at the moment of their birth and multiple people at the moment of their death. In every instance – sickness, health, life or death, I have observed how the aura reacted and how it felt: how the colors and patterns changed, how the light grew brighter or dimmed, how afflicted areas of the body looked and felt differently than the parts that were whole and healthy.

I know the energy centers are real because I can see them spinning like omnidirectional tornadoes of power emanating beyond the body. After decades of observation I have been able to correlate, in many cases, health problems in the body with changes in the speed, color and size of the corresponding energy center.

This is not a special ability of mine. As I teach extensively in my book ***Auras: How to See, Feel & Know***, anyone can use simple exercises to train the rods and cones in their eyes to be able to see auras. I have just been doing it for a long time, so my repository of knowledge about what it all means is fairly

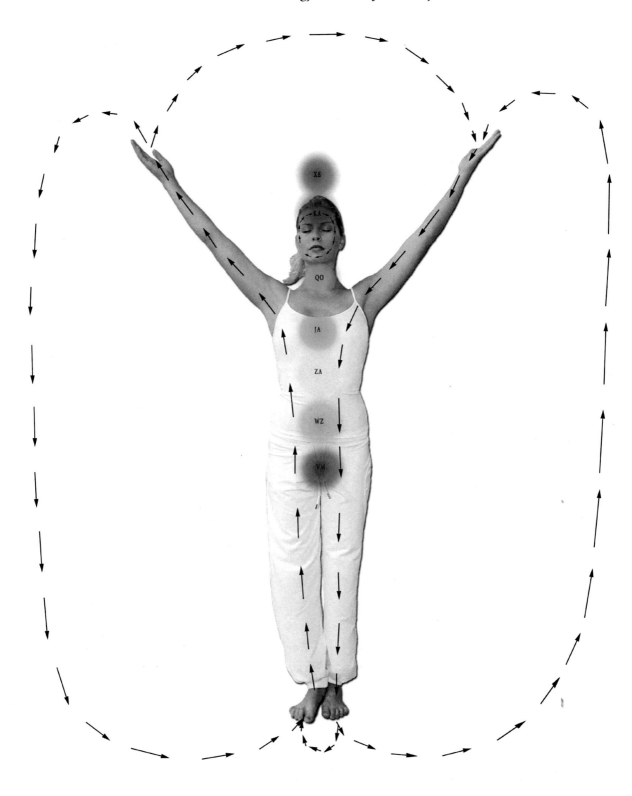

Energy Flow in the Human Body

deep.

The ultimate use of the knowledge of the energy centers and energy flow in the body is two-fold. First, it can be used to diagnose energy blockages or disruptions that may be contributing to physical, mental or emotional problems. Second, energy can be applied from another person to specific areas to release blockages in an afflicted person or revitalize energy flow that has slowed, thus allowing their body to have more power to heal.

In extreme instances, where the energy practitioner is releasing a large amount of bioenergy into the afflicted person, miraculous healings can occur. In the early 1980's, Dr. John Zimmerman, from the University of Colorado School of Medicine, used a SQUID Magnetometer in a series of scientific studies to measure the bioenergy released from the hands of energy healers. His studies showed an enormous pulsating release of biomagnetic energy whenever they used their abilities.

Zimmerman's findings were confirmed in 1992 by studies of Seto in Japan. Along with colleagues, he studied energy healers and found that in many instances they could produce enough Qi energy from their hands to be measured by a standard two coil magnetometer.

Why are the Body's Energy Centers Important?

From a health standpoint the energy centers are immeasurably useful in both diagnosis and healing. Returning to the theme of this book, there is a third very helpful use of observing the energy patterns of people. With couples, it is easy to see and feel which energy centers they connect on because there is an obvious reverberating resonance between the centers. Is their relationship purely sexual? Or does it go deeper and thereby hold the promise that it will be more long lasting, by showing a connection to the mind, heart and other energy centers? This will be explored in detail in later chapters.

A Little History

Most people, if they are aware of a system that distinguishes the energy centers of the human body, are probably somewhat familiar with the popular Chakra system, which has Hindu origins. Somewhat less known is the similar Tree of Life system followed in Kaballah that originated amongst the Hebrews. There are other, less known philosophies used to describe the energy centers of the human body as well. Though they all refer to the 7 major energy centers they have different beliefs and teachings as to the exact location, significance and function of those centers. Nor do some systems limit themselves to 7 energy centers, with as many as 12 being referred to in some philosophies. While many place them in front of a body, others use the back, or some point halfway in between. It is not simply a matter of the different philosophies calling them by different names.

The most popular energy center beliefs in the western world are based on the Hindu teachings of the Chakras, which originated thousands of years ago in India. 'Chakras' are frequently bandied about these days among the enlightened of the western world, though for most, without a true understanding of the origins, or the depth of insight the energy centers have to tell.

The Chakras and other human energy center philosophies, correspond somewhat in location and basic color to the more accurate and detailed Root Ki body energy system explained in *Celestine Vibronics*. In essence, The Root Ki, Chakra, Kaballah and most other systems all correctly identify the approximate location of 7 key energetic areas of the body. From a physiological standpoint, the 7 energy centers occur over the 7 main nerve ganglia of the spinal column.

Other than this chapter, throughout this book the energy centers of the body will be referred to by the two letter *Celestine Vibronics* Root Ki designations of Xe, Ka, Qo, Ja, Za Wz and Vm. This is both for simplicity of nomenclature and exactness of purpose, as revealed by the physical evidence of a person's aura, rather than by a particular belief or philosophy.

Chakras are mentioned as psychic consciousness centers in yoga texts as early as 600 BC. The western world was first introduced to the concept of Chakras and energy centers in the body with the publication in 1919 of the book The Serpent Power, by Arthur Avalon. This book was a translation of three important Indian texts: the Padaka-Pancaka from the 10th century gives descriptions of the body energy centers and practices for using them; the Gorakshashatakam, also from the 10th century, details instructions for meditating upon the Chakras; lastly, the Sat-Cakra-Nirupana, from 1577, contains instructions from an Indian guru on use of the Chakras. These texts are the foundation for modern, western understanding of the Chakras as well as the basis for Kundalini yoga.

There tends to be some confusion about the various systems of identifying the energy centers, even within a single system such as Chakras. Part of the problem is some systems look at the back of a person and others the front, with correspondingly different names. Additionally, there are many pictures and illustrations of the energy centers on the Internet and they often use different nomenclature and assign different purposes to the energy centers.

These pictures always assign specific colors to each energy center respectively. However, the colors assigned are far too simplistic compared to an actual aura and seldom the true color of the energy center at any particular time. The actual auric colors are not constant, but vary in size, color and density depending upon the energetic health of that area.

The picture below shows the seven energy centers with the most commonly associated colors, as well as the varies nomenclature associated with each center by the multiple teachings, beginning with the Hindu Chakras on the far left, followed by western variants and ending with the Kaballah on the far right. The names for the energy centers using the most accurate Root Ki system are shown within the colored spheres on the body.

This chart is merely for illustrative and educational purposes to show the approximate locations of the energy centers and their common names in the various systems, as we will be using the swirling centers of power a lot as we explore the energy dynamics of Soul Mates. The reality is the colors, size, and opacity are almost always different than a monocolor. The one time the simple, traditionally depicted colors are useful, is helping to visualize and focus on an energy center when you are seeking to re-balance and re-energize it.

Keep in mind that the six systems shown, with their accompanying names, in many instances assign completely different meanings to the energy centers, and have different methods, philosophies and objectives when they are working with them. Nor are they the only systems out there that assign

Sahasrara	Crown	XE	Seventh	Crown	Kether
Ajna	Third Eye	KA	Sixth	Brow	Hokmah
Vishuddha	Throat	QO	Fifth	Throat	Binah
Anahata	Heart	JA	Fourth	Heart	Gevurah
Manipura	Solar Plexus	ZA	Third	Navel	Tifferet
Swadhisthana	Sacral	WZ	Second	Sexual	Yesod
Muladhara	Root	VM	First	Base	Malkuth

meaning and names to the energy centers. In CV, the system I use, the Vm is the lowest energy center and the location of the sexual and creative energies. The purpose now is simply to familiarize you with the location and colors generally assigned to the energy centers, along with common names you may hear them referred to elsewhere, so you have a point of reference when they come up later in the book.

I love you not only for what you are, but for what I am when I am with you. I love you not only for what you have made of yourself, but for what you are making of me. I love you for the part of me that you bring out.

~Roy Croft

When you can't believe your eyes,
you can always trust your heart.
Love makes anything possible.

~Unknown

A soulmate is someone to whom we feel profoundly connected,
as though the communicating and communing that take place
between us were not the product of intentional efforts,
but rather a divine grace."

~Thomas Moore

Chapter 4

TWIN FLAMES OR SOUL MATES?

The relationship terms Twin Flames and Soul Mates are used interchangeably by many people. But energetically they are different. There is also a prevailing, though not universally shared sentiment, that a person only has one Twin Flame or Soul Mate. After six decades of personally observing auras and the interaction of auras between couples, as well as my own experiences in relationships, I can confidently assert that each person has many, many Twin Flames and can even have more than one Soul Mate. I know that is a sacrilegious statement to some people. But it is the reality of what I have seen and experienced by observing the energy connections between couples.

While a Soul Mate relationship always has a romantic foundation, a Twin Flame relationship may be entirely platonic and also with someone of the same sex, even among people who are not gay.

It is both easy and wise to look at your current or prospective relationship and determine whether they are Twin Flame or Soul Mate in nature, or of the more common variety. Taking romance out of the equation and just assessing your energy connections with friends to see whether any are Twin Flames, can also be quite revealing.

Take a closer look at the seven major energy centers of the body and what they represent as you assess your romantic connections.

A very short casual relationship, including one night stands and brief flings, will most likely only have a strong connection to the Vm, the sexual energy center. Due to cultural or religious constraints the relationship itself may never enter the bedroom, but the connections with the Vm still burn with passion.

A short-term relationship, one that will likely last from a couple of weeks to a few months, will tend to have a Vm connection between the couple, plus another energy connection between them to one of the six other energy centers. Which other energy center can be quite varied. It will be one where they have some level of common ground. It will usually be the heart center of the Ja. But if they think similarly they may be connected on their mental centers of Ka. Or, if they are both very active physically they connect on their energy center of Wz.

XE

KA

QO

JA

ZA

WZ

VM

A long-term relationship will energetically connect on three to four energy centers, which can be varied. While some will eventually end in separation, it is often after years and only occurs once they have grown apart with their interests, faith and/or goals diverging on separate paths.

However, it is not uncommon for strong relationships that connect on three to four energy centers to maintain lifetime relationships, especially if both have a personal commitment to continually nurture their relationship, focusing on what they continue to have in common that bonds them, and not upon what they do not.

One of the important aspects of successful relationships of this type is for both people to acknowledge that their partner has some interests and needs that they do not fill and to be trusting and supportive of them pursuing those other activities and passions on their own or with other people. This is true for Twin Flame relationships and even for Soul Mates. Though more energy connections will equate to more common interests, it will never mean that a couple, even the most loving, connected and devoted couple, shares every interest and entertainment preference. That would end up not only being pretty boring, but also stifling of personal, individual growth by limiting exposure to other people with their varied personalities, quirks, knowledge, interests, wisdom and relationship dynamics.

When a Twin Flame relationship exists there will be energy connections on five or six of the seven primary energy centers. If the relationship is between close friends, two people of the same sex that are not gay, then the Vm sexual energy center will usually be the energy center where there is no connection; but not always. The Vm is also the energy center of creativity. Though it is unusual to find in heterosexual Twin Flame relationships of the same sex that are friends not lovers, they could still have an energy connection between their Vms if it was creative in nature, such as two people that have a love for creative expression in activities they shared together.

Given the nature of true Twin Flame relationships, an average person will likely encounter three to six in their lifetime. If they are extroverted and meet many people, they will probably encounter more. Some will be prospective mates, but many of both sexes will just have the potential to become very close and trusted friends in a relationship that fulfills and resonates on many levels.

Soul Mates are manifested when a couple connects on every major energy center. That doesn't mean they are mirror images of one another. It does mean they have a tremendous amount in common, particularly their core energies. They will be on mutually harmonious spiritual paths; likely come from similar cultural and educational backgrounds; have some common recreational interests; have harmonious personalities that are mutually respectful and seldom clash or argue; fulfill each other physically and sexually; and inspire and encourage one another to expand.

More importantly, they will be each others best friend and see both the present and the future in the same way. In the present, they will likely be similarly alined politically as well as in their religious beliefs. They will have common lifestyle preferences: if one is fine with a middle class income so will the other be. Alternatively, if one likes big homes, fancy cars and a ritzier life, it will be true of the other as well. If one likes life in the big city or out on a rural farm, their partner will match their desire.

Looking into the future, whether it is how many kids to have and how to raise them, where to live, what type of education or profession to pursue, where, when and how to retire, or what big legacy goals to pursue - in all major areas Soul Mates will find common and harmonious ground. Their high level of compatibility and common likes and dislikes, is created by a combination of their similar formative upbringing, their mutual interests, and the harmonious connections between each of their primary energy centers, which enables them to think and feel similarly on a wide range of subjects and interests.

Unfortunately, some people meet their Twin Flame and even more so their Soul Mate, and do not recognize them for who they are. It seems incredulous that this could be so, but it is not uncommon, even when people are actively seeking their Soul Mate. There is only so much energy to go around between two people. The greater number of the seven energy centers that connect harmoniously the less energy there is for each one. This sometimes results in a person not experiencing the exhilarating rush of passion with their Soul Mate that they do with someone with whom they connect on only one or two energy centers. Without that passion rush, a Soul Mate may be overlooked as just a very comfortable friend, while another person that perhaps connects only on the sexual (Vm) center and the heart (Ja) becomes the an intense love and relationship interest.

Think about it like this: suppose all the energy available between two people was represented as 100 energy units (EU). In real life, a person can choose how much energy they give to any particular energy center at any particular time. But for this example, as Soul Mates are connected on all seven energy centers, let's assume that all are getting equal energy. This means 100 EU divided by 7 = gives each energy center approximately 14 EUs. Fourteen for the heart center, fourteen for the sexual center, fourteen for the center of the mind and onward to each one equally.

On the other hand, along comes a person who only connects with the heart and sexual center. They may only have a total of 50 EUs to project. But as their energy is only divided between two energy centers, the person on the receiving end is getting 25 EUs to their heart center and 25 EUs to their sexual center. That compares to the Soul Mate who is spreading 100 EUs among 7 centers and is only sending 14 EUs to the heart of their prospective mate and only 14 EU's to their sexual center. So even though the receiving person of the two-center connection is getting less total energy, it feels like more because it is concentrated in just two energy centers, especially when it is concentrated in the heart and sexual centers , which are the two most "feeling" centers..

It should become obvious that for the person on the receiving end, a burning passion may be created for the person from whom they are receiving 50 EUs to both their heart and sexual centers. It is easy to fall madly in love with such a person, even though they are the completely wrong person! A relationship founded on only one or two energy centers will not last, for there is no common ground in the other energy centers to maintain an interest in one another beyond the bedroom. Frictions arise because of the incompatibility in the other energy centers. And it is connections in the other energy centers that sustain relationships when they are stressed by the challenges of life, as all relationships eventually are.

So what is a poor Soul Mate to do when their prospective Soul Mate connection doesn't recognize them and instead is infatuated with someone else who is only connecting on their heart and/or sexual center, but giving them a great big blast of energy to those centers? All you have to do is remember that you are the master of you. As you command your body, it will obey your commands.

Remember the above example of 100 EUs divided equally between 7 energy centers was only an example. In real life, though you are harmoniously connected to your Soul Mate on all 7 energy centers, it is *not* necessary for you to give equal energy to each one. Especially during the courtship time, when you are perhaps competing with other suitors, don't be hesitant to focus more of your energy into your heart, and if appropriate your sexual/creative center, or whatever center is your Soul Mates passion. There will be all the time of your life together to explore the intricacies of your other energy centers. First, you have to win their heart today, so there is a tomorrow together.

One other surprise about Soul Mates: another sacrilegious reality -- there's no guarantee it will always be so. Every person evolves over time. As they learn new things, discover new interests, lose old ones, react to traumas and challenges, gain or lose religious faith, they change. Nobody at 60 is the same person, with the same likes, dislikes, passions, faith and interests as they were at 20. They will still have some continuity from 20 to 60, but they will have also shed some aspects of themselves and taken on new traits, habits, interests and often the way they think and feel spiritually. As they evolve as a human being their personality will also change over time. When they were young they may have been idealistic and spontaneous. Life's challenges may have ground them down to cynical and boring. Alternatively, like my father, they may have been prejudiced and domineering when they were in young, but evolved to color blind, fair and patient as they experienced more of life.

Ideally, Soul Mates evolve on similar paths. While this is far more likely with Soul Mates than it is with any other type of relationship, it is still possible for Soul Mates to evolve apart. Even when that is the case, they will likely remain together because, even if they devolve into Twin Flames they will still have far more energy connections than most couples, which will continue to make it pleasurable and fulfilling to remain together.

One other interesting note: you can have more than one Soul Mate! Although it is rare, it can occur, although not at the same time, as someone in the fulfillment of a current Soul Mate relationship would simply not be energetically open to discovering and making connections with another. Though this fact also goes against the romantic conception of Soul Mates, it is inconceivable that in a world of a millions of possible mates that there would not be more than one that has harmonious energy connections with you on all seven of your major energy centers at any particular time.

Human energy is always in flux. All of us are continually evolving and changing. So the common notion that Soul Mates are forever, even remaining constant from lifetime to lifetime, only holds true if the couple remains in close enough contact to continue to evolve together along common paths and doing so continues to be a passionate desire of both of them.

The good news is even when Soul Mates grow energetically apart they are so close to begin with that they will likely still be Twin Flames and still have an outstanding and fulfilling relationship.

It works the other way as well. A couple that begins their relationship as Twin Flames could evolve in time into Soul Mates. If their love is strong and they share a mutual desire to bring happiness to the other; continue to share and expand common interests; and are open to exploring new facets of themselves, they will likely become closer energetically and evolve into Soul Mates!

There may be a million things to smile about, but you're definitely my favorite one.

Unknown

A soulmate is the one person whose love is powerful enough to motivate you to meet your soul, to do the emotional work of self-discovery, of awakening.

~Kenny Loggins

Chapter 5

THE SOUL MATE LOVE GRAPH

The course of a typical relationship, one that is not between Twin Flames or Soul Mates, can be plotted on a graph with reliable accuracy. Normal relationships almost invariably follow the same path.

When the relationship is new it is on an upward slant; everything is still being discovered about the

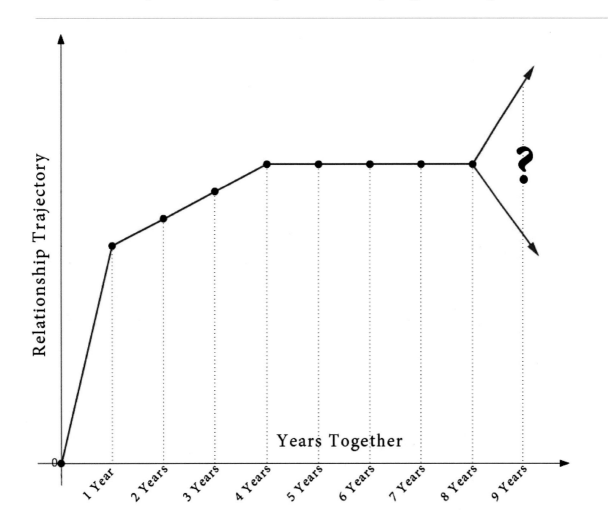

other person. Some of it may not be interesting or attractive, but for the most part the very newness of the relationship and joy of discovery is exciting and can even be euphoric. A person wants to present their finest behavior during the early courtship mode. They tend to hide their deficiencies and magnify their best qualities. Because of this, new relationships often motivate individuals to forsake or lessen their bad habits and make concerted efforts to magnify their good traits. In the process, for a time they become the best person they can be in many aspects of their life. In this sense, new relationships, when they are founded upon love, often become catalysts for personal improvement and expansion.

Over time the upward slant of the Love Graph decreases. It still goes up, but at a reduced angle as the newness of a relationship fades and the everyday habits and peculiarities become entrenched. This can be as short as a few days for people who are not energetically compatible, to months or a couple of years for couples who are more compatible in interests and energy, to several years for two people who have many common connections.

Eventually, the line of the graph plateaus. Depending upon the depth of the original love, the strength of the energy connections between the couple and the variety of common interests and goals they share, as well as each person's personality, the time until the plateau can be weeks to many years. But eventually it happens, even in the best of relationships; even in Twin Flame or Soul Mate relationships if they have neglected to continue to nurture and cherish them.

A plateau is the most crucial time in a relationship. If a couple recognizes it for what it is and takes joint action to reinvigorate their relationship, then the line of the graph will once again resume an upward course, signifying that being in the relationship is continuing to help fulfill and expand both individuals.

Sadly, more often than not, a plateau is the point the couple realizes they are bored with each, no longer have much in common and have ceased being catalysts for each others growth and happiness. Over time, though they both have continued down the path of life, they have diverged down different paths of personal growth and grown apart as a couple. Perhaps one became more spiritual while the other did not walk that new path with them. Perhaps one radically changed their diet or their friends and the other was still caught up in the old habits or friends. It is not uncommon at all for one person in a relationship to evolve spiritually, ethically and in habits and interests, while their partner is still stuck in the rut of the past and likely happy to still be there.

It can also be the case where the pressures of life, work or family dynamics, changes the habits and even character of one person in a relationship in a negative way. For example, perhaps they entered their relationship as a very light, occasional consumer of alcohol, only to become a heavy drinker as the pressures of work, finances and/or family challenges weighted them down.

For whatever reason, at some point in almost every relationship that is neither a Twin Flame or Soul

Mate connection, a couple realizes that being together no longer contributes to their fulfillment or personal growth. In fact, often just the opposite: it is taking away from their happiness and diminishing their personal growth.

Being on a plateau is like being balanced level on a teeter-totter: the slightest movement will propel you either up or down, depending upon what movement you initiate. It is the same for couples who find themselves at their relationship plateau. If they still have an abiding love for one another, are still close enough energetically, still have enough common interests, goals and spiritual and lifestyle choices, they can use their continued connections as a foundation to recommit themselves to expressing their love by word and deed. They can choose to once again be inspirations and catalysts to bring out the best in one another: to motivate, inspire and propel each other to greater heights in all aspects of life. They can honestly examine their lives and identify the places that have become blockages and vow together to blow them up! They can recommit to strengthening their bonds by taking actions that reinvigorate their relationship and bring back the old feelings of love, respect and even awe for their partner.

Or, as many people who find themselves on a plateau, they realize they have drifted so far apart and have so little still connecting them that they would be better off apart. They may not act upon that inner knowledge right away, because of concern for children in the relationship, finances or other factors. But they will know the truth in their hearts and the line of their Love Graph will drop off the plateau and begin its downward plummet. It is not a matter of if the relationship will end, just a matter of when.

This same graph can still reflect couples who are Twin Flames or Soul Mates. But downward spirals are much less likely to ever occur. When plateaus are reached, there is almost always sufficient energy, common interests and lifestyle connections remaining that it is very likely that the couple will take the actions necessary to resume an upward track on their Love Graph, embodying personal expansion and growth stimulated by the dynamic love energy of their relationship.

Given the understanding that a relationship that begins as a Twin Flame or Soul Mate is much more likely to last and continue to reward each person with love, fulfillment, personal growth and expansion, it just makes sense that every effort should be made to seek out and enter this higher type of relationship, rather than waste time on one that will be less satisfying and more likely to end down the road.

In the coming chapters we will explore the three ways you can determine how energetically connected you are to your mate or potential mate: seeing your energy connections; feeling your energy connections; and deductively ascertaining your energy connections if you can neither see or feel them.

My soul has been searching for you and even though you are miles away, when I close my eyes, I feel you in every breath I take, we were meant to be together as one for all of eternity.

~Karen Kostyla

Whatever our souls are made of, his and mine are the same.

Emily Brontë

You are the sun in my day, the moon in my night, the spring in my step, the beat in my heart, the love of my life. You are my everything and I love you with everything I am.

~Unknown

~ ♥ ~

Chapter 6

HOW TO SEE AN AURA

An aura is a bio-electrical field that exists and emanates from all living things. In plants the auric field is typically two layers. In humans, it is seven layers. The first layer, begins appearing as a translucent distortion of space, like heat waves on a hot asphalt highway and is quickly perceived by most people after just five minutes of eye exercises. Each succeeding layer is increasingly challenging to perceive and requires more dedication and time devoted to the eye exercises and practice looking at auras on as many people as possible.

In aura classes I have taught during the last two decades, people who have never seen even a glimmer of an aura, usually are seeing the first layer within five minutes. Many people are seeing the second layer within another five to ten minutes of practice; it's that easy. It doesn't take any special psychic ability, just a knowledge of how to accomplish it. However, there are some serious misconceptions about auras.

Kirlian photography is often thought to create photographs of auras. It was accidentally discovered in 1939 by Semyon Kirlian, and refers to a photograph made possible because of the application of high voltage in the process. Kirlian discovered that an object resting on a photographic plate and connected to a source of high voltage showed a thin corona discharge along its edges and surfaces. Kirlian himself asserted that these were pictures of the auras. But the fact that the same images appear when the process is applied to inanimate objects such as a coin, tend to discount the likelihood that these are actual pictures of the aura. Scientific investigation has concluded that the images are corona effects similar to those produced by a high voltage corona seen with Van de Graff generators or Tesla coils.

Now there will be some who will argue that Kirlian photography or the Aura Photography I will talk about next, really are photographs of auras. But as someone who has seen auras since my childhood, I can tell you the real thing is much more magnificent.

Another popular form of "Aura Photography" is often found at psychic fairs and produces colorful pictures that show a person engulfed in various opaque colors that extend out from the body several inches. These are also not true pictures of auras, but are made with a special camera that interprets galvanic skin responses and then adds the appropriate colors using a printer. It's like a mood ring for your whole body. Aura cameras do not use high voltage as the Kirlian method does and no direct contact with the photographic film is made.

Now let me put you on the road to actually seeing auras quickly. When you focus on anything there are components of your eyes called rods and cones that change shape to render the focusing. All of your life your eyes have been habituated to using their rods and cones in just a few simple ways to see things close up and to see things farther away. By using a few easy exercises you can quickly train your rods and cones to stretch and contract in unfamiliar ways that will allow you to see auras. As a side benefit, many of my students have reported improved vision once they started exercising their rods and cones.

Auras also incorporate more than the visible light your eyes have been accustomed to seeing your entire life. Below is a chart of the electromagnetic spectrum. Visible light is only a very small part of the spectrum. As you successfully retrain the rods and cones in your eyes you will be able to see other parts of the nearby spectrum.

The easiest place to see an aura is around someone's head as that is a powerful location of bio-energy emanations. It's best to have them stand near a dull white wall, in normal indoor room light. Do not

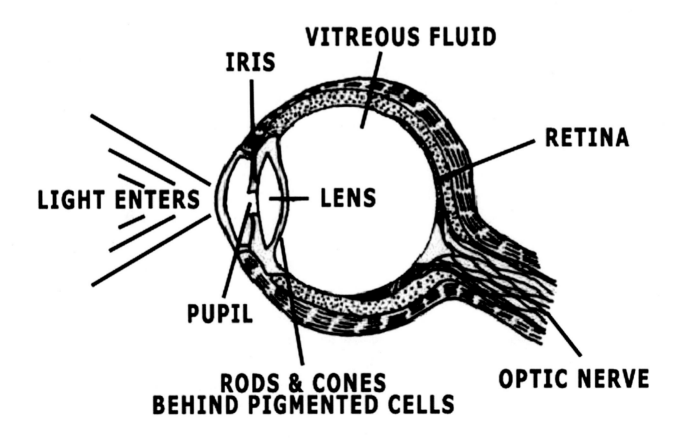

Anatomy of the Eye

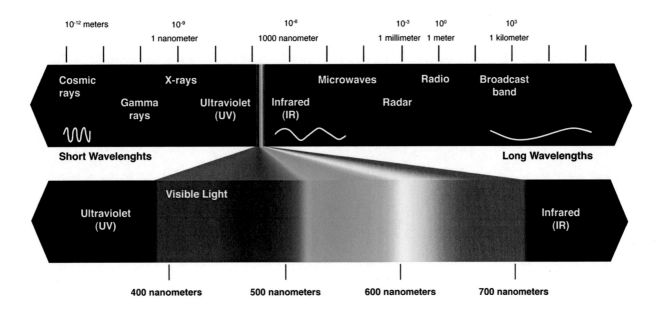

Electromagnetic Spectrum showing thin band of visible light

focus on their face, but aim your gaze toward their forehead or tip of their nose, look through them as if you were focusing on a point on the wall directly behind their head. At first you will just see a translucent distortion of the space around their head, kind of like heat waves on a blacktop road on a hot summers day. But there will be no doubt that you are seeing something you have never seen before!

As you continue to gaze through them and see the first layer of their aura, it will begin to change from translucent to opaque white. Keep looking. As the rods and cones in your eyes continue to adjust, more colors will begin to appear further out from the head.

Be patient. It just takes some minutes for your eyes to adjust to the new settings that are being implemented. It's similar to when you first go from a light room to a darkened room. At first you cannot see anything in the darkened room. But after a few minutes your eyes begin to adjust to the darkness. The rods and cones in your eyes stretch and constrict to allow your eyes to see better in the darkened environment.

If you remain in the darkened room for a half hour you will be amazed at how well you can see in the dark after you've given your eyes time to readjust to the vision that is being asked of them. It is the same with seeing auras. Though most people, with vision in both eyes, can begin seeing the first aura layer in five minutes, if you continue looking you will begin seeing many more layers and colors that are visible after fifteen to thirty minutes of observation.

As you become perfected in your ability to see auras you will be able to see the sublime seventh and final layer. It is really an astoundingly beautiful and captivating sight unlike any other aura seen among

Layer 1 of the Aura

plants or animals. Seeing the seventh layer certainly instills a belief that humans are far more than they imagine.

60

Layer 7 of the Aura

Here are a few of the most popular eye exercises from my aura classes:

Exercise 1: Not sure if *your* eyes have what it takes to see auras? Here's a quick, simple exercise to prove the rods and cones in your eyes will realign in the way necessary to see auras. Standing in front of a window that looks outdoors or a distant wall in the room, hold a pencil or pen *vertically*, centered about 1½ to 2 feet in front of your face. Focus on the pen or pencil. Now look past the pen or pencil and focus

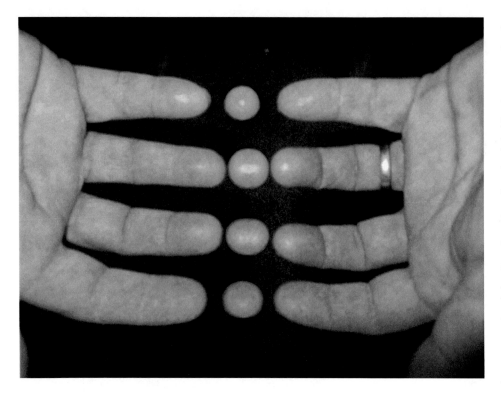

out the window at whatever object is 10- 50 feet away like shrubbery or your next door neighbor's house. Immediately, with your focus in the distance, you will notice that the pencil close to your face now appears to be two pencils! Though this is an optical illusion it does prove that the rods and cones in your eyes **will** refocus as needed to see auras. The secret of seeing auras is very simple: *observe what is close while focusing through it and upon something more distant.*

Exercise 2: The Floating Fingertips is an amazing little illusion that helps retrain the rods and cones in your eyes to see auras. Sit in a short-seated chair over a carpeted floor. Turn your hands palms up, resting your forearms on your legs. Touch each of the fingers to the corresponding finger on the other hand. Now look past your fingers and focus your eyes on the carpet below. While maintaining your focus on the carpet, slowly pull your fingers apart about ¼ of an inch. You'll immediately notice that you now have a new set of magic fingertips floating between your fingertips on each hand! Have fun with this one.

Exercise 3: In this exercise simply put your hand with fingers splayed apart against an off-white or lightly colored wall in a room with a normal level of natural or artificial light. Look at your hand, but focus through it to the wall beyond. Now slowly move your hand up and down a few inches either direction. Within a couple of minutes, often within just a few seconds, you will begin to see the first layer of the aura with the translucent, distorted space close to your hand and in between your fingers.

Exercise 4: The Ultimate Aura Trainer: The invention of Magiceye 3D pictures created the single most effective tool for learning to see auras. When your eyes refocus in the manner necessary to see the 3D image you have just used your rods and cones in the exact manner necessary to begin seeing auras. When you see a 3D picture you are looking at something that is close, but your eyes are focusing on something that is farther away, beyond the object you are actually looking at. That is the exact technique for seeing auras.

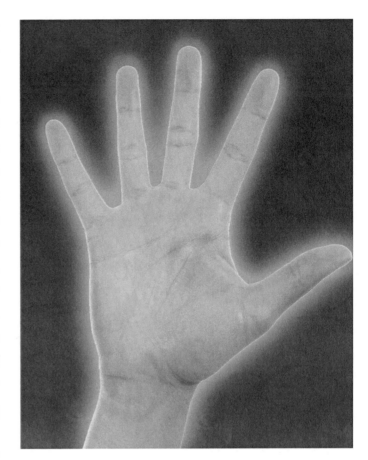

Although there are many other eye exercises you can do to help retrain the rods and cones in your eyes, including those in this book, all of them pale compared to Magiceye 3D pictures. I cannot emphasize enough that doing your eye exercises with the Magiceye 3D pictures will help you not only see auras quickly, it will help you see them in vivid colors and far greater detail than any other method you employ in your training. If you do no other eye exercise except learn to see Magiceye 3D pictures within an instant of looking at them, you will be well on your way to becoming very proficient at seeing auras in full, vibrant color.

Time after time in *How to See Auras* classes I have taught, there would always be students who struggled to see more than the thin opaque white auric outline after concluding the basic eye exercises. But once they successfully could zoom in to the Magiceye 3D pictures, they immediately began to see auras in wispy, pale colors and the world of seeing auras truly began to open for them.

An Internet search for Magiceye 3D pictures will find several sites where you can view a wide variety of Magiceye 3D pictures.

Here are links to a few good ones:

www.magiceye3ds.com/pictures.aspx?page=1

www.magiceye.com/

www.vision3d.com/sghidden.html

If you truly want to see auras in fullness and in vivid color, please visit these sites and incorporate viewing and seeing Magiceye 3D pictures for at least 15 minutes each day. This is the fastest method to retrain the rods and cones in your eyes to see auras. With some people, one 15 minute session is all they need. Other people may need several sessions before auras are seen in color and fullness. Persist until you succeed. As long as you have vision in both eyes, even if it's terrible vision, you will succeed if you persist. The longest I've known someone to persist until they achieved success is 16 fifteen minute sessions. So even if it's challenging for you it should not take that long before you are having great success seeing auras.

You should know that your eyes will not be damaged by viewing Magic 3D pictures. In fact, just the opposite, as eye specialists use Magic Eye 3D pictures for vision therapy. Think of viewing Magic 3D pictures as Zumba for the eyes.

If you are viewing the Magic 3D pictures on your computer, to insure eye safety, maintain a normal distance from your monitor screen and remember to blink normally.

In addition to helping you be able to see auras, according to the Magic Eye websites, Magic Eye 3D pictures are also useful for "improving vision, relaxing the body and calming the mind."

To have the Magic Eye 3D picture "pop" into view simply focus through the picture. You can do this most easily by picking a single, tiny spot near the center of the image and from a distance of a foot to two feet, focus solely on that spot. Fairly quickly the 3D picture should pop out. Once the 3D picture becomes visible the longer you look at it the sharper the image will become. Once it is in focus you'll be able to move about in the picture, viewing different aspects and locations.

If you have a passion to learn to see auras in their full glory as scintillating jewels of rainbow light, I encourage you to get my book Auras: How to See, Feel & Know. This book has been #1 on multiple Amazon category best-selling lists since 2012. It includes detailed explanations of the colors you can see and has comprehensive instructions, including 17 aura-seeing eye exercises and *47 **full color*** photos and diagrams to help you fully see the magnificent, beautiful world of auras!

The minute I heard my first love story I started looking for you, not knowing how blind I was. Lovers don't finally meet somewhere. They're in each other all along.

~Rumi

No measure of time with you will be long enough, but we'll start with forever.

~Edward Cullen

My love for you has no depth, its boundaries are ever expanding.
My love and my life with you will be a never ending story.

~Christina White

Chapter 7

HOW TO FEEL AN AURA

Auras can be felt as well as seen. What may at first be invisible to your eyes until you retrain your eye's rods and cones, will usually be able to quickly be felt with a couple of simple exercises. The feeling can occur as a physical sensation such as hot or cold, a thickening of empty space, tingles both pleasant and the kind when one of your extremities falls asleep from having blood flow cut off and is painfully waking up. It can also be an intuitive feeling such as knowing a person is sad even if they never spoke or gave an indication that it was true. Empathy is a third way to feel an aura. In this case, as you approach someone and your auric field interacts with theirs, if you are a sensitive empath, whatever they are feeling will suddenly be your feelings as well.

The easiest way to begin learning to feel auras is to start with your own.

Exercise 5: Hold your hands with fingers pointing out, palms facing each other and hands spread about one foot apart. Close your eyes and think about feeling the space between your hands. Like retraining your eye's rods and cones, giving any thought to the feeling of the space between your hands is probably something you have never done or even considered. But you will be able to feel that space. Your body has the inherent ability to feel auric fields including your own. Everyone can do it. This is not a special ability, just a matter of allowing yourself to become sensitive to something you have never thought about doing before.

With your eyes remaining closed, slowly bring the palms of your hands toward each other until they are only a breath away from touching. Then slowly move them apart again.

Repeat this action several times, in and out. You will begin to feel something as you continue to move your palms toward and away from each other. What you feel varies from person to person. Commonly, people feel a thickening of the space between the palms. Hot or cold sensations and tingling feelings are also frequently experienced.

As you repeat the action you may orient your hands in different directions while maintaining the palms parallel to each other.

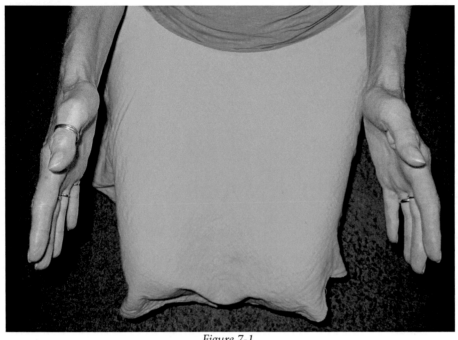

Figure 7-1

If after several movements back and forth you haven't recognized any physical sensations between your palms, imagine a large rubber ball like the red ones the school children play with, being held between your hands. Now push in and out just a few inches, while picturing the squishy ball. Continue practicing until you are feeling physical sensations between your palms.

Most people will begin feeling distinct sensations with any of these physical exercises within 30 seconds to a minute.

Exercise 6: With your left arm bent at a 90 degree angle, as shown in figures 7-3 through 7-5, point your right index finger at the middle of your left upturned arm or palm, holding the tip of your right index finger about one inch above your left upturned arm/palm.

While remaining pointed above your left arm/palm, and with your eyes closed, begin moving your pointed, right index finger in random movements above your arm/palm.

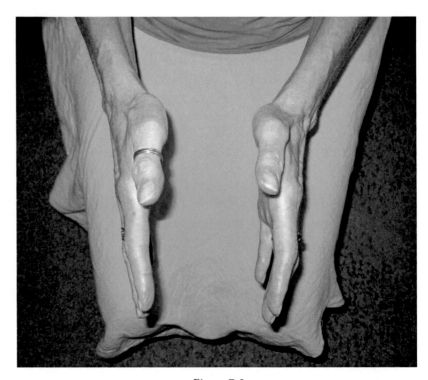

Figure 7-2

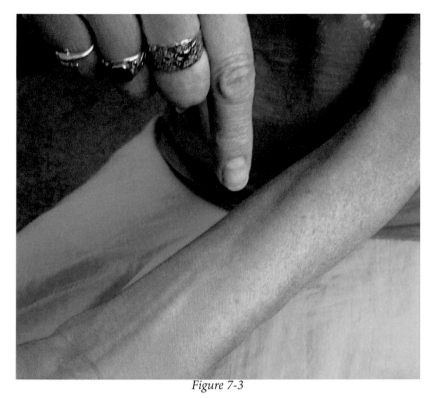

Figure 7-3

Though your eyes are closed and your index fingertip is not touching your arm/palm you will quickly be able to feel the scribing motion of your pointed finger on the surface of your upturned arm/palm. For some people it may be as in the previous exercise, a thickening feeling, hot, cold or tingles. For many people it feels as if the tip of a lead pencil or pen is moving across their arm/palm and many are incredulous to open their eyes and see their right finger is truly not touching their left arm/palm.

Just as your palms were sensitive areas when learning how to feel your own aura, the same holds true for feeling other people's auras.

Exercise 7: Find a partner and stand facing each other about two feet apart, as shown in figure 8-1, with your elbows close to your body, and your palms held up vertically. One person's right palm should be directly opposite the other persons left palm, separated by about 1 foot of space. Close your eyes and focus on feeling the space between your palms and the other persons. Keeping your eyes closed, move your palms slowly

Figure 7-4

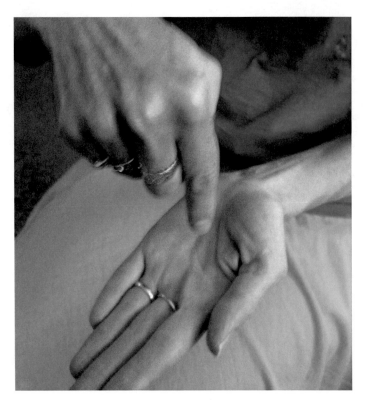

Figure 7-5

toward the other persons palms without actually making physical contact. Then slowly move your palms away from one another. Continue to repeat several times and note the physical sensations you feel between your palms as they move toward and away from each other.

WHEN I TELL YOU I LOVE YOU, I DON'T SAY IT OUT OF HABIT. I SAY IT TO REMIND YOU THAT YOU ARE THE BEST THING THAT HAS EVER HAPPEND TO ME.

~UNKNOWN

If kisses were a tree, Id give you a forest. If hugs were leaves, Id give you a tree. If love was water, I would give you the ocean.

~ Unknown

Chapter 8

WHICH IS BETTER SEEING OR FEELING?

I am often asked which is a more accurate measure of a person; to see or feel their aura? The answer is feeling is actually more accurate, but seeing is much easier to learn unless a person is naturally very intuitive.

When you see the colors, holes and vortexes in an aura, you learn over time, after you correlate body language, spoken words and obvious physical or emotional symptoms, to trust that the things you see are sure indicators of what you have determined them to be. But that depth of knowledge cannot be written in a book because there are far too many variables. You cannot simply say that a certain color means a certain thing. For instance, you may see the color red around a persons head. It could mean they are excited, or angry, or passionate, or mentally unstable, or have a life threatening tumor in their brain. Which one it is would need to be determined by looking at other parts of their aura and assessing other symptoms and indicators from their actions to their words.

Trying to understand what is going on with a person solely from looking at their aura is not unlike a doctor trying to figure out the root cause of a mystery disease. There are many factors, aura and otherwise that need to be considered to make an accurate assessment.

Feeling an aura on the other hand can be refreshingly clear. Regardless of whether you intuitively, empathetically, or physically feel a persons' aura, the end result is you instantly have a very clear and exceptionally accurate understanding of their current physical, emotional and mental state. You may not know the cause of the problem at first, but you will be clear on its manifestation.

Returning to the example of a person that is sad, you may know that intuitively, or because you felt the dark shudder of sadness, almost like the aura is crying, when your aura interacted with theirs. Or, if you are also naturally empathetic, you will start feeling sad yourself once your aura is touching the other persons. But after all that knowing, you will still be unaware of the cause of their sadness until you make more observations and/or speak to the person to garner more information.

However, teaching someone to feel an aura is not nearly as easy or successful as teaching someone to see an aura. The basics of seeing can be taught in five minutes. Students can begin seeing the first white opaque auric field just minutes afterward. Feeling auras through one of three common means is fairly easy for people that are naturally intuitive and empathetic. People without those traits in abundance have a greater challenge. Instead of instantly knowing with a high accuracy, what the aura is telling them, they will flounder in bewilderment, unsure of what they think they are feeling, and even doubtful of whether they are really feeling anything or just imagining it.

Yet, with feeling being the most accurate method to understand what another person's aura is telling you, it is worth working on the ability to feel auras by practicing the exercises in the previous chapter.

When the angels ask what I loved most about life, I'll say you

~Unknown

You know you're in love when you can't fall asleep because reality is finally better than your dreams.

~Dr. Seuss

~♥~

Chapter 9

HOW TO USE YOUR AURA
TO FIND YOUR SOUL MATE

This chapter is for those who have succeeded in seeing or feeling auric energy. You do not need to be an expert experiencing all the layers and nuances of auric fields. But you do need to have confidence that you can sense and perceive auric energy either by feeling or seeing. If you are not yet there, you can proceed to chapter 11, which will give you a method to locate and identify your true Soul Mate even if you can neither see or feel auras.

The first big task in finding your Soul Mate is figuring out where to look. Is it someone you already know? Someone you are currently dating? A friend or even a casual acquaintance or a co-worker? Or, is it someone you have not even met yet?

If it is none of the people in your immediate life, neighborhood or work place, is it someone way off somewhere in the great big world, perhaps even in another country?

Here are the energetic steps to follow to find your Soul Mate. Be sure to speak aloud your questions and always refer to them as "my Soul Mate", and never by "he" or "she." Saying "Soul Mate" coalesces the energy much more than the simple pronouns.

1. Determine if he/she is someone you already know or a stranger.

1a. For this you will require a candle, preferably a wide squat one with a single wick. A long skinny candle is actually the most sensitive, but can more easily give false signals due to wayward breezes. A purple wax candle works best. If you cannot find a purple one, green is the next best color. If neither of those are obtainable a white candle is another option.

1b.You will also need to get a piece of white poster board or white cardboard that is thick enough to stand up on edge without bending and falling down. Using a black marker, write "Soul Mate" on the board.

1c. Light and place the candle on a small table that you can sit close to and can have the edge of the table opposite of you up against the wall.

1d. As upright as possible, lean the poster board with Soul Mate written on it against the wall opposite of where you are sitting, so it is facing you with the candle in between.

1e. Hold your hands up on opposite sides of the candle flame, with palms facing each other and spaced about one foot apart.

1f. Try not to disturb the natural vertical flame by breathing out on the candle flame or moving your hands rapidly near it.

1h. Your aura is moving powerfully between your palms and through the candle flame. If there is a change in your auric energy the flame will indicate the change in numerous ways, which can include, unaccounted flickering, flame suddenly leaping up, flame suddenly goes out, flame starts spitting, heat of the flame increases, or flame or smoke changes color or opacity.

1i. While looking at the words "Soul Mate" written on the board opposite you, and holding your hands, palm facing with the candle flame in between, one at a time ask each of the possibilities for the location of your Soul Mate. As you ask each question slowly bring your two hands closer to the flame until they are only separated by about 3 inches and you can feel the heat of the flame.

Continue to ask the next series of questions until you get an affirmative answer.

Q1. Is my Soul Mate someone that I know? (If "no" proceed to 2. If "yes" proceed to Q2).

Q2. Is my Soul Mate someone I have known for a long time?

Q3. Is my Soul Mate a close friend?

Q4. Is my Soul Mate just an acquaintance?

Q5. Is my Soul Mate someone I have dated?

Q6. Is my Soul Mate a co-worker?

Q7. If you received negative answers to questions 1-6, feel free to formulate additional questions to help determine how you know your Soul Mate.

2. If you determined that your Soul Mate is someone you have never met, you then need to do the same procedure as above to determine where this person is. They could be anywhere in the world. It kind of becomes like the game Twenty Questions (or more) as you narrow down the location by getting positive answers to the earlier questions.

For example: Is my Soul Mate an American? (yes) Does my Soul Mate live in the United States? (yes). Does my Soul Mate live in Alabama? (no) Does my soul Mate live in Alaska? (no) Does my Soul Mate live in Arizona? (yes) For the next set of questions go alphabetically through the cities and towns of Arizona to determine which one your Soul Mate lives in. Does my Soul Mate live in Apache Junction? (no) Does my Soul Mate live in Avondale? (no) Does my Soul Mate live in Benson? (no) Does my Soul Mate live in Bisbee? (yes)

At this point you have options depending upon how much you want to find your Soul Mate at that moment in time. If the place they live is a small town like Bisbee, population 5,575, I would recommend traveling there and using your auric attraction to locate your Soul Mate, which I will explain below. If they live in a larger city, I would recommend looking at it on a map and marking off sections (section 1, section 2, sections 3, etc.) The bigger the city the more sections you will need. Each section should have a population of not more than 30,000, unless you are very aura sensitive, in which case you could go with a larger number as you see fit.

Once you have arrived in the small town or section of city, you should plan on spending at least a week and mingling as much as possible everywhere you can from stores, to events, to parks, to church, to the supermarket! Pay particular attention to attending every event or activity that is of interest to you. Remember, your Soul Mate will have most of the same interests that you do, so it is more than likely that you will encounter them at one of these activities or events.

Once you actually are within sight of your Soul Mate, you need to either see many energy cords going from your energy centers to theirs, or to feel a magnetic attraction to them that is not purely a physical attraction. In fact, there may be little physical attraction at all initially. The attraction you feel will be of two auras in complete resonance. When this occurs, both auras light up and expand, even if logically or from a physical attraction stand point, it would not seem to be a person you would be strongly attracted to. Remember, initially you will probably not feel the intense passion you have with lesser people, because the energy of your aura is divided among all the energy centers of your Soul Mate, not just focused on the heart and sexual/creative centers.

Verifying Your Soul Mate

In your search for your Soul Mate it is quite possible you might meet someone who is a Twin Flame. You may also meet someone to whom you have strong heart and sexual/creative connections that are so potent, you get caught up in the moment and forget all about looking for your Soul Mate! But if you are determined to settle for nothing less than your Soul Mate, you need to aurically test every person you feel might be the one. This is a test that must be done in person, facing each other about six feet apart, without any distractions such as periodic kissing, hugging or talking. You must have a willing partner for this last step, even though it would be wise to not tell them exactly what you are doing, lest they try to influence the results.

a). As you are standing about six feet apart facing each other look up to the other persons psychic center (Xe) which is right above their head. Continue to look at their Xe until you either see or feel it's energy.

b). Once you see the other persons Xe energy, look for the energy cord that will be running between your Xe and theirs. If you do not see one, they are not your Soul Mate. If you are better at feeling then seeing auric energy, you can sense this energy cord. Again, if you sense nothing, this person is not your Soul Mate.

c). If you see or feel some connection with your psychic energy centers you can proceed to the next

81

energy center of the mind (Ka) and give it the same scrutiny and test. The connection does not need to be extraordinarily strong. It just needs to be present at a reasonable level, not just a tendril or absent.

d). As long as you continue to show positive connections, continue going through all of the energy centers in a similar manner. If you get through all seven primary energy centers with positive responses on each one, you have found your Soul Mate!

FOREVER IS NOT A WORD...RATHER A PLACE WHERE TWO LOVERS GO WHEN TRUE LOVE TAKES THEM THERE.

UNKNOWN

*True love spreads forth its arms when two hopes meld
into one dream, when unconditional love is reciprocated
unconditionally, when love for the beloved
is as important as love of self,
when the hands of two lovers clasped tenderly together with
reverence and thankfulness jointly open the fabled door.
When each gives all to the other, both win everything.*

~22 Steps to the Light of Your Soul

~ ♥ ~

Chapter 10

BODY LANGUAGE OF COUPLES, LOVERS & SOUL MATES

In your search for your Soul Mate you will likely have other relationships along the way. Body language is a good way to know when things are going right or wrong in your romantic relationships. If you have already used your aura to find the person you feel is your Soul Mate, body language is a great second opinion to verify what your energy connections have told you.

And even in the very best relationships there will be stormy times and bumps in the road. Being aware of couples body language helps you quickly realize when life challenges are negatively affecting your relationship so you can consciously act to change the energy and restore a loving harmony.

Relationship experts have asserted that courtship behaviors, both accepting and rejecting, are far more non-verbal than verbal. People can deceive easily with suave words, but body language tells no lies. In relationships, we communicate more with the nuances of our bodies and eyes than we do with our words. According to anthropologist David Givens, 60 to 90 percent of communication in normal human interaction is non-verbal. With romantic couples, it can shoot as high as 99 percent.

We consciously speak the words that come out of our mouth. But the signals and messages our bodies, eyes and facial expressions convey are subconscious. We think of what we are going to say, but not of 'how should I hold my eyebrow to convey my desire?' Because body language is spontaneously and innately expressed without premeditated thought, it is a much surer way to know the truth of someones feelings or intentions. Intuitively, we give more credence to the body language if it is at odds with the words being spoken. To Paraphrase Emerson, "What you are doing is shouting so loud, I cannot hear the words you are speaking."

Given this reality, having a good understanding of common body language seen among couples can be an eye-opener. Whether you are a novice at seeing auras or an expert, also taking a moment to observe the body language between you and a romantic interest is an invaluable confirmation. Body language can be a confirmation of their true feelings, and oftentimes the depth of their love.

Contemplate the evidence of the sixteen couples body language questions below and compare it to your own relationships both in real time, while you are interacting, and reflectively as you recall your interactions. How deep is your love? How deep is your partners? Does your relationship hold long term promise? Or is it likely to end quickly? The answers to those questions and many more can be found in the body language between couples and are a great addition to seeing and feeling auras, to help assess your romantic relationships.

Many of these questions and answers can take place simultaneously in the context of a single moment.

If you want to keep score (optional) rate your relationship with each of these questions on a scale of 1 (lowest) to 10 (highest). A perfect score would be 160.

1. Lingering, loving gazes: *At least several times during the day when you are together, do you and your companion look into each others eyes with lingering, loving gazes?*

Explanation:

In normal human interaction, people have a strong urge to avert their eyes within 3 seconds of making eye contact. The more people are in disagreement, dislike each other, or feel intimidated in the situation, the shorter the eye contact will be. When people are very uncomfortable in another person's presence, eye contact may be avoided all together.

Loving, harmonious couples on the other hand, love to look into each others eyes. Looking deeply

for a lingering time into your lovers eyes is a powerful, emotional connection. It can even seem to cause your heart to skip a beat! As the years pass, if the flame of love continues to burn inside and isn't subdued by the challenges of life, this distinctive body language signal will continue to be exhibited.

Warning Signs:

The more strained and less loving a relationship is, the less couples will make eye contact. If the relationship is on automatic pilot, where they simply go through the motions every day without passion or desire for one another, they will tend to look at each other the same way they look at other people, with short, quickly averted glances. If the relationship is souring and there is palatable tension between them, they will tend to look through each other. Though it may seem to observers that they are making eye contact because they are looking at one another, perhaps even while talking, they are in fact not looking into each others eyes.

Ways to Improve:

If you are experiencing lack of meaningful eye contact with your love partner and desire to nurture your relationship back to a better level, you will need to make a conscious effort to make eye contact with them and hold it in a caring and loving way. If they avert their eyes, even when you are trying to hold theirs, it might be necessary to reach over and gently hold their head between your hands so you can maintain your eye contact. This is simple but powerful relationship medicine. Loving eye contact reaches into a deep emotional well of good memories and positive energy connections. It can bring a disgruntled companion into a peaceful space where the relationship has an opportunity to reset in a more positive way.

2. Eye Crinkle Smile: *When your beloved flashes a smile at you, whether silently or in conversation, does the outside corner of their eyes crinkle into crows feet?*

Explanation:

A fake, insincere, or half-hearted smile is made with the lips only. A happy to see you, or hear your voice smile, crinkles the corner of the eyes into crows feet. This is an especially valuable telltale of true feelings or intent as it is one of the most difficult body language signs to fake. Even con men, who may be experts at mimicking body language signals to fool their victims will likely miss this key indicator.

Officially known as a "zygomatic smile," it cannot be produced on demand like blinking your eyes if you desire. This is a heartfelt, upward smile of pure emotional happiness, which contracts muscles in the cheeks strong enough that the smile travels up to the eyes and causes little crows feet wrinkles to momentarily appear.

The face muscles are directly connected to visceral nerves, which react strongly to emotions, making the face the most intricately expressive part of the human body. Think for a moment how many feelings and emotions can be expressed with nothing more than a facial expression.

Warning Signs:

The eye crinkle smile should be something you are frequently seeing with your beloved or anyone close to you. If not, it is a good indicator that the relationship needs some tender loving care.

Ways to Improve:

A good place to start is communication together. Find out why the relationship may not be as fulfilling for both of you as it should be. If both people want the relationship to improve, they will both be open to discovering and eliminating the frictions.

3. Eyebrow Flash: *Do you and your partner often share eyebrow flashes?*

Explanation:

Couples with a good love rapport feel a deep 'oneness' with each other. It is a higher level of feelings than they have for anyone else. If they have been together for any time they also develop a comfortable familiarity with each others personalities, quirks, thoughts and emotional states. This is often reflected in subtle glances and eye contact, very slight nods of the head and most commonly in quick eyebrow flashes when they look at one another.

The eyebrow flash, where one or both eyebrows are momentarily spontaneously raised while making eye contact, is a positive recognition sign, often used to convey either an 'are you thinking the same thing I'm thinking?' or a flirtatious love message, such as 'hey there beautiful', or simply a private acknowledgment of a love connection with no other message intended or implied.

Warning Signs:

Eyebrow flashes actually happen fairly frequently between couples with a base of love and good rapport. Seeing one from your partner is an unconscious lift to your spirits.

In relationships where they are lacking or not demonstrated because of tension between the partners, it can be a significant contributor to unplaced feelings of sadness.

Ways to Improve:

The eyebrow flash is usually a completely involuntary reaction of the body to connect on a personal level with someone, particularly a loved one. Being consciously aware of facial body signals allows you to

make efforts to be more expressive in your facial expressions, particularly when you are communicating verbally or non-verbally with your loved one.

4. Attentive Head Tilt: *When you are in conversation with your companion, particularly when you are alone, does he/she tilt their head to the side periodically while talking and listening to you, particularly when listening?*

Explanation:

Even a slight lean of the head in either direction toward the shoulders sends a message of, "I'm interested and at peace with you." This body language indicator holds true for everyone, from kids and parents, to unknown people at social gatherings, to couples and lovers. Between couples or lovers, it is a flirtatious, warm, strong energetic signal of sincere interest on multiple energetic levels. Among parents and children it is less seldom seen as it indicates the kids are actually listening and interested in what the

parent is saying. In a social setting it is a way to show sincere interest and non-verbally send a non-threatening reassurance.

The muscles initiating the head tilt are similar to the shoulder muscles, which hunch and tense, or relax, as they are subconsciously prompted by visceral nerves, which are stimulated by emotion.

Warning Signs:

When couples speak to each other, especially in private and do not show the head tilt, it is indicative of friction, disharmony, or emotional disconnection in the relationship. The head tilt sends a soft, loving signal. Lack of the head tilt during a conversation between couples, shows someone that is energetically disconnected, either in disagreement with what the other person is saying, or simply doesn't care.

Ways to Improve:

Make a conscious effort to listen and be interested in what your partner is saying. Even if you are having a disagreement, control your emotions, stay calm, and sincerely listen to what your partner has to say. Don't tune them out while they're talking because you are mentally busy preparing your retort.

5. Attentive Listener: *When you speak to your companion are they attentively listening?*

Explanation:

Couples with good energetic connections listen with sincere interest and attention when their companion is speaking directly to them. They make regular eye contact, are receiving and processing what is being spoken, periodically nod their head in agreement or understanding and involve themselves in the conversation at the appropriate moments without interrupting in the middle of the other person's speech.

Warning Signs:

Failure to make regular eye contact and calm, meaningful, vocal responses.

Attention focused on something else other than the person speaking, such as watching TV, reading a magazine or doing something on their computer or cell phone.

Interrupting, not letting the other person finish what they are trying to say, and especially speaking over them in a louder voice.

If you are talking about a sensitive subject, they may avoid your gaze and fidget in their seat or frequently touch their face, their ears, eyes, nose or lips as a non-verbal way to disregard what you are saying or indicate that what they are replying is not true.

If you are in an argument or disagreement when your companion has done something wrong, watch for signs that are insincere, such as trying to make you feel guilty and that it's your fault. In many situations, both parties have contributed to creating the problem.

However, if you clearly know that your companion instigated and caused the problem, but they are so unwilling to face the reality and are trying to turn the tables to make you the guilty party, watch out. This is a strong sign of a controlling and manipulating person that is poison to a long-term relationship.

Other signs of a manipulator is someone who is unwilling to take responsibility and sincerely listen to your concerns, or someone who never answers your questions directly, but instead either asks you a question, or gives a long-winded, irrelevant reply, or asks a question while simultaneously putting themselves up on a moral pedestal, such as, "Why would I do that?"

Ways to Improve:

You cannot control your companions actions, but you are the master of your own. Hopefully, you'll grow together by mutually looking at unproductive behaviors and jointly agreeing to make personal efforts to improve your relationship. When your companion is speaking to you, whether it is about something trivial or important, give them your attention. Make eye contact and listen to what they are saying. Give them appropriate responses and especially verbal support along with hugs or touches

if they are sharing problems or challenges they may be having.

6. Sitting Close: *When at home or out socially, do you and your partner choose to sit wherever, which oftentimes may not be near each other, or do you both make conscious choices to sit next to one another? When you are alone at home together, how often do you choose to sit close enough that your hips touch? If you are sitting opposite, but close to each other, do you allow your feet or knees to touch?*

Explanation:

Couples with strong emotional connections and fulfilling relationships draw supportive energy from each other and tend to sit close to one another whether at home around the dinner table, out socially at a restaurant, or at a get-together with friends. Especially at a table with many other people from kids at home to friends in a restaurant, couples that are in a loving, mutually beneficial, harmonious relationship, often without forethought will choose to sit near each other, either side-by-side or kitty-corner. The exception of course is in social settings where there are assigned seats, or the sexes are segregated with the girls and guys grouped separately.

Even if you can't see auras yet, it is a fun exercise to go to a restaurant and look at couples. Whether they are alone together or with a group of friends, it is pretty easy to spot the couples that have strong bonds and a fulfilling relationship together just by looking at their body language and how close they are sitting to one another.

Another good telltale is how close they sit if they are side-by-side on a couch. Do they keep a space separation between their bodies or do they have contact at their hips? If they are sitting opposite each other do they make foot or knee contact with one another?

Couples in love, or even those who are meeting for the first time that have a love chemistry, will be almost magnetically drawn to be near to each other when they are in the same room. They may not have even asked for a first date yet. But their instinctual desire for proximity, along with other body language signals will be broadcasting their heartfelt interest.

Warning Signs:

Never sitting close in social settings and very seldom at home is an indicator of an emotionally distant and energetically disconnected relationship. If you make a conscious choice to bridge the gap and sit next to your partner, even hip to hip and they move away to put more distance between you, it is obviously a very strong indicator of relationship discord.

Ways to Improve:

It is interesting how simply making a conscious choice to sit next to your partner, even hip to hip, can create closer energetic bonds between you and your mate. While observing the negative body language can indicate problems, consciously initiating the loving behavior can nurture frayed bonds and instigate more love and affection in relationships where there is still hope for a future together.

7. Mirroring: *How in sync are you and your partner? Do you get up and go to bed at the same time? Do you like the same recreation and entertainment? Do you enjoy the same foods, especially share the same menus for meals? Do you have common levels of spirituality and share the same religious views? Are you on the same page for having and raising children? Do your personalities have many similarities*

or many opposites? Are you complementary and non-competitive in your professional lives? Are you both happy with how the other dresses? Do you like the same type of people for friends? Are you both introverts, extroverts, or opposites? Do you aspire for the same goals for the future, both for your relationship and where you see your lives socially, economically and in lifestyle, 5 years, 10 years and 20 years down the road?

Explanation:

Couples that have strong connections on many of their energy centers are very similar in most, if not all major areas of their lives. This helps bring about a deep sense of comfort and security in the relationship. Harmony abounds as the couple agree on so many aspects of life, there are few topics remaining to get in disagreements or arguments about. The synchronicity in close relationships is often so pronounced that if they are in a room full of people and one of the partners takes a sip from their drink, the other will soon follow. If they are alone together, it can be almost simultaneous.

Anthropologists call this unconscious mimicking of behavior "isopraxism," from the Greek iso meaning 'same' and praxism which means 'behavior.'

Isopraxism is very common among both humans and animals, particularly during courtship and among strongly bonded couples. It is very commonly observed among birds, especially parrots, most notably in the mutual head bob. One will initiate it and keep doing it until the other mimics it. Once they are in synchronicity, it establishes them as a non-threatening safe member of the flock. If they have amorous intentions it opens the door to further actions of affection and courtship behaviors.

Warning Signs:

Take note of the synchronicity in your own relationship. Do you begin and finish meals together? Do you have shared routines, including when you do household and yard chores? If you have children, where do you sit in relation to them at the table? Not only is it an important question for you, your seating arrangement makes a subconscious impression on them as well. If you sit at opposite ends of a long table it sends the message that there is a lack of closeness between the parents and likely a clash of wills.

Ways to Improve:

Choose to sit closer more often. Give your companion more smiles and compliments of appreciation. Make efforts to develop an interest in entertainment and recreation areas you may not currently be involved in together. In any and all aspects of your life that you are not close, where you do not mirror each other, give a mutual effort to better understand and try out the activities that captivate the other.

"The more alike you are, the more you like each other," Givens says. "It strengthens your bond."

8. Love Voice & Tone: *Does your companion speak to you in a different, softer tone of voice than they do with any other person?*

Explanation:

Lovers have a way of speaking to one another, both in person and on the phone that is softer, more affable and energetically connected than with other people. With both men and women, the voice tends to be a slightly higher pitch and have a warmer tone. It is not loud, harsh, or have any negative inflection. We register tone more strongly then the words themselves. If someone says, "I love you," without true feeling and energetic connection, the other person will know that the words were insincere.

Warning signs:

The tone of voice alone can convey love, anger, disapproval, hate and any other emotion. Compare how your companion speaks with you and how they speak with others, both in person and on the phone. If they speak with you just like they do any other casual person, but with close friends and especially prospective other suitors they speak in the higher, warmer, more laughing and flirtatious voice, they are showing an energetic disconnect from you and a stronger energetic connection to the other person.

Ways to Improve:

Work on your relationship in every positive way you can. The love tone of voice or lack of it, is really just an indicator of the health of a relationship. If you try to change it alone when you are speaking to your companion, it will seem contrived. If your relationship improves from the many other positive actions that you and your companion take, then the voice change will occur on its own.

9. Heart Hugs with Full Body Accompaniment: *Take notice how you and your partner hug. Do you hug with your head over each others right shoulder or left shoulder? Are your bodies making physical contact at your chest, stomach and groin?*

Explanation:

There are three ways people hug and this act alone can distinguish whether they are lovers, friends or merely acquaintances.

The energy centers of the body come into play very strongly when people hug. In normal interaction people keep an unconscious space between them as they talk and work. But when they hug, this barrier is momentarily broken and their energy centers completely interact and overlap. But even in this, people will still put up unconscious barriers to protect their energy centers.

Completely without thought, when acquaintances hug they will not allow their bodies to touch other than as little as possible at the upper part of the chest. They will also almost always embrace with their head over each others right shoulder. Casual friends will also usually hug each other in this manner.

If they are warm friends, they will still hug each other in this manner, but they will unconsciously put their heads over each others left shoulders.

If they are close friends, they will unconsciously put their heads over the others left shoulder and will also allow body contact down to the stomach area.

If they are a couple or have romantic interest in each other, they will embrace with their heads over the left shoulders and unconsciously have full body contact from the chest down to the groin area.

This strange, unconscious behavior is not governed by culture or social norms, though they can have an influence. The main force creating these unique and very predictable postures is the interplay between the energy centers of two people.

It all begins with the heart. A hug with each persons head over the others left shoulder allows their chests to be positioned so their heart energy centers are in closest proximity. A hug with heads over the right shoulders does not bring the heart energy centers as close, even if their chests are still touching.

An embrace that includes contact down to the navel area, is one that brings more energy centers into closer proximity and is only seen by people who actually feel closer to each other than casual acquaintances.

Lastly, lovers or those with serious romantic interest in one another, will make a tighter, full body contact, starting at the chest and continuing down into the sexual areas of the groin.

Warning Signs:

If your partner does not automatically embrace you with their head over your left shoulder and contact down to the navel with every hug, and full body embraces at least sometimes during the day, your relationship is not energetically well connected emotionally.

And a big warning sign is if you see your partner embracing anyone else with a full body embrace!

Ways to Improve:

Interestingly, if you consciously insure that your embraces are over the left shoulder and make contact at least down to the navel with every embrace and down to the groin as frequently as possible, you will be activating energetic resonance between your energy centers and your partners. It's like jump starting a stalled car, or in this case, a stagnating relationship. Even if you are having obvious problems and coldness in your relationship, full body hugs, loving eye contact and warm, full smiles, can circumvent your challenges and reconnect you energetically on an emotional and Soul Mate level.

10. Daily Kisses of Greeting and Parting: *Does your partner kiss you goodbye with sincere affection every day when you part for your separate daily work and activities? Do they kiss you with the same obvious love fairly promptly when you are first reunited later in the day?*

Explanation:

One of my strongest memories from childhood, a ritual I grew up determined to emulate in my adult life, was watching my mother and father kiss with obvious love and joy every single day when my Dad would leave for work and every single day when he would come home. No matter how tired or difficult his day may have been, coming through the entry door the first thing he would do is look to find my Mom. All the cares of work written heavily on his face and weighing on his posture would vanish in the moment of his embrace and kiss with my welcoming mother.

This is not a perfunctory peck on the cheek or lips. While usually a quick kiss, it is still preceded by loving eye contact. The kiss itself is with softened lips that are warmed by the love between the couple. A quick kiss of love like this is a relationship reassurance that in parting says, "I love you and if I didn't need to go to work, this would be a lot longer kiss." And in returning home, "I love you and have missed you and the greatest balm to my challenging day is your warm embrace and sweet kiss."

Warning signs:

Unless it is culturally taboo, no kiss at all when leaving or coming home should be a big warning sign of a relationship that is emotionally restricted. But it may not be as automatic for some people as it was for me, if they did not have the good example of two loving, emotionally open parents to emulate. If the hello/goodbye kiss is given, it should be with soft lips that are often warm with love. If the kiss ends up being a peck or especially if it is against hard lips that stay tightly closed instead of parting and inviting, it is a relationship that still needs to become more emotionally connected.

Ways to Improve:

The morning kiss is easier. The day hasn't unloaded the weight of a lot of problems on either partner yet. Make a conscious effort to make lingering eye contact before your kiss, then open your lips a bit to give a soft, loving kiss. If your partner is a bit uptight and closed lipped, reach up and gently put a hand on each side of their neck to express love and release tension; then kiss them again.

Returning home in the evening, each of you may have had challenging, even nerve-wracking days. This may be especially true for a stay-at-home Mom who's been trying to herd a pack of chaotic kids around all day. Despite it all, make a commitment to always greet each other with love and sincere, heartfelt affection, even gratitude to be back in one another's embrace after the trials of the day. If you do have children at home, I can assure you from first-hand experience, that seeing the parents express that kind of unwavering, 'you are my heaven' type of love is a huge security and wonderful life example.

11. Matching Smiles: *Does your companion smile when you smile, especially in social settings when*

you are standing or sitting together with other people?

Explanation:

Couples in harmony smile in unison at each other. It sounds corny, but it is completely an instinctual sign of closeness that demonstrates affection and enthusiasm in the couples emotional connection and commitment and pride in the relationship and for the mate. Especially when a couple is standing or sitting together talking with family or friends. If they are in harmony in their hearts and minds it shows in their mutual smiles of respect and love when they look at one another. This subconscious behavior is readily observed during introductions, especially to people who you are meeting for the first time, or to close family or friends who are meeting the mate for the first time. At those key times, a person in love is proud of their mate, and feels good subconsciously taking the opportunity to 'show them off, to publicly demonstrate their 'couplehood.'

Warning Signs:

If a couple is together with other people and one smiles at the other but the sign of affection is not returned, it demonstrates friction in the relationship, or a relationship energetically out of sync and harmony, especially if it is during an introduction to other people, or during activities within a larger family group, or when they are speaking together with each other. This can become very pronounced when visiting the family of one of the partners. Happy, in harmony mates, put each other up on pedestals, even more so when they are around family. They let their family know by their eye contact, smiles and inclusiveness with their husband/wife/companion/lover that there is a special bond, affection and loyalty that is at the highest level.

Insincere, forced smiles don't count. They are evident by their strained, tightness that they are contrived to put on an appearance for the moment and do not reflect the behind the scenes reality. A true smile involves many muscles of the face. A true smile 'lights up the face' and it is the whole face that smiles, not just the lips. With contrived smiles the face remains rigid and impassive in contrast to the lips that make a smile.

Ways to Improve:

As this is an automatic action given without thought or intent, it is not something that can be improved upon directly without seeming insincere. The only way to improve it is to work indirectly by other actions that bring the relationship closer, energetically more in sync and harmony.

12. Walking Together with Body Contact: *Do you and your partner walk together often? Whether a walk in the park or entry to a social gathering, are you side by side? Especially if you are in a private setting like a stroll on the beach, do you walk together and at least part of the time hold hands or interlock your arms around each others waists, or the man with his arm over the woman's shoulder?*

Explanation:

Couples in love, the ones that feel the love in their heart, not just think of it in their mind, are drawn to walk together and to make light, affectionate, physical contact with one another while they are walking. It promotes a comfortable sense of relationship security and oneness.

Warning signs:

Couples that consistently walk apart, especially one ahead of the other, and even more so when that distance widens, are demonstrating a lack of connection in the energy center of their heart. This is also manifested when one of them decides to make a stop in a place of business, or a sudden change of direction, and does so without any communication, verbal or nonverbal, with their partner. This type of behavior shows they are quite disconnected energetically and likely behave the same at home or in social settings.

Ways to Improve:

Make a mutual choice to hold hands while you walk. If there are children in tow, put them on the outside of the parents who are holding hands in the middle.

13. Holding Live Hands: *When you and your companion hold hands, are your hands unmoving like holding a dead fish? Or are they animated with frequent little affectionate movements and gentle squeezes?*

Explanation:

Regularly holding hands is a good first step. But heart connected couples will share frequent, small, movements that telegraph "I love holding you and being here with you." An occasional squeeze, swinging the arms while looking into each others eyes, or a movement of the fingers to allow a gentle stroking of the palm of the hand with the fingertips are commonly seen by couples in love.

Warning Signs:

Quite simply, how often do you and your companion hold hands? When you do, is it without feeling, not really different than holding a book, a mannequin, or a palm size fish?

Ways to Improve:

Make a conscious choice to hold hands

regularly and to not just have limp, unmoving hands. Give a love squeeze every now and then. Occasionally untangle your interlocked fingers and gently stroke your partner's palm or the inside of their lower arm with your fingertips.

14. Peek-a-boo, I Want to See More of You! *Do you ever play adult peek-a-boo with your partner?*

Explanation:

Many of us remember the childhood game of Peek-a-boo I See You! One person lifts their head to spy on the other with their eyes showing the lower part of their face hidden, then quickly hides their eyes and entire face only to suddenly reappear with another peek-a-boo. It is guaranteed to bring a smile to your face and likely some laughter, especially when played with small children.

Adults can play this game too and it can often lead to adult rewards! Perhaps you are sitting in the same room both reading a book or magazine. One of you looks toward the other than covers your face. Hopefully they'll notice. Do a peek-a-boo with just your eyes showing above the top of the magazine and see if they are looking at you. If they aren't, clear your throat in a pleasant, attention getting sort of way. Once they gaze over at you, give them a quick eyebrow lift that silently says, "hello beautiful", or "hi handsome", then duck back down for another peek-a-boo hide.

Round two can just be a peek-a-boo to remind them that you are thinking about them. Or, if you want to add some sexy "come hither" looks, it could be the opening invitation leading to more intimacy

with a spice of levity.

Warning Signs:

Adults can often get mired down taking life too seriously and letting the daily grind and responsibilities suck all the fun out of it. This is a state that can be very detrimental to relationships. It is easy to become too adult in our thoughts and behavior and too forgetful of our inner child and how to just have simple fun and laughter.

Ways to Improve:

Peek-a-boo is a great little exercise to release your inner child giving him or her permission to come out and play. It all begins with making the choice, the decision, to stir up your relationship in a playful way.

15. Cuddling: *How often do you and your companion cuddle? Do you cuddle sitting together? Laying in bed together just talking? Only in private, or also in social settings?*

Explanation:

Cuddling is a good indicator of couples that are energetically close to one another. Cuddling can be done standing, walking, sitting or laying down together. It can be a private moment, or occur around others in a social setting. Any close body contact beyond holding hands can be considered cuddling: heads touching, shoulders touching, walking arm in arm, hips touching, legs intermingling, snuggling one behind the other, encircling the inside person with your arms.

Couples that are close to one another in their energy and harmony naturally are drawn to cuddle at some point every day. In socially restrictive or inhibiting cultures this may only be when they are alone together in bed. In more open cultures among couples still enraptured in their relationship, some form of cuddling will occur multiple times during the day.

Warning Signs:

If you and your partner never or very seldom share any cuddling behavior, look back on earlier times in your relationship. Did you cuddle more often in your first months or years together only to see it wane or even disappear over time? If so, it is an indication that you have energetically drawn apart. Body language such as holding your hands clasped together, especially behind your back, can also shout that you do not want to cuddle or get physically closer.

Ways to Improve:

As with every relationship improvement, it begins with an honest assessment that something more than the status quo is needed to reinvigorate the relationship. That acknowledgment, preferably from both partners, needs to be followed by a conscious decision to alter your behavior to affect a change. Ideally, this is something couples talk about and make joint decisions to change and improve the way they relate to each other and express their love.

16. Light, Loving Touch:
Does your companion lightly and sensually touch you with their open palms and fingertips during the day, particularly in spontaneous acts that may take only moments, such as passing you when moving about, or with a quick loving embrace while stroking your neck or forearm?

Explanation:

The same hands that can perform hard labor can turn into

sensual, titillating organs when softly touching a lover. Romance in movies use the hands to convey love very well as seen most memorably in the movie "Ghost" when Patrick Swayze cupped Demi Moore's hands as she was working with the wet clay on a spinning potters wheel.

We have been trained from birth, when our mothers tenderly rubbed their palms against our baby cheeks, to feel a sense of love and security when we receive a gentle touch with warm palms and fingertips; doubly so when it is accompanied by eye contact. Known as 'palmar touching,' this simple act of unspoken, unconditional love is a tremendous pacifier and bonding action between mother and child. It is the same years later between couples in love.

The love touch usually involves both the palm and fingertips. Sometimes it is firm and other times gentle, but it is always warm and loving. It may be a gentle touch on the inside bare forearm, along the sides of the neck or on the inner thigh, stroking the head and hair, massaging the neck or forehead, even rubbing noses! It is not uncommon for it to send tingles through the bodies of lovers when it first occurs. It is a potent bonding trigger, especially when it is bare skin upon bare skin.

Medical researchers have noted that the love touch releases the hormone Oxytocin in the brain, which acts to induce and reinforce pair bonding. Loving hugs alone can have a similar effect, but the love touch tends to be a more powerful stimulator of the 'love hormone,' especially when it is combined with a hug. Researchers have also noted that tenderly touching those you care about and the subsequent hormones that are released, benefit our physical, mental and emotional health. The opposite would then also logically be true: lack of tender, loving physical touch in a relationship can be a detriment to ones physical, mental and emotional health.

A variation of the love touch is a fingertip caress. My wife tells me she has "arm orgasms" whenever I ever so lightly stroke the inside of her forearm, and experiences tingles up and down her spine when I run just the tip of my fingernails very, very softly up and down her back and neck. Fingertip touch is very personal. It reinforces a strong bond and a special relationship.

Touch is one of the most telling yet subtle body language actions. Not just where one person touches another, but also how and how long. Love touching subconsciously is done with a relaxed hand and open palm with fingers gently spread. The touch is not quick and gone, but lingers like the warm sun on a long summers day.

Warning Signs:

When a relationship becomes emotionally disconnected there is little if any palmar love touching. Touching becomes infrequent and most often just with the fingertips. And then only as a way to get attention and not meant to convey love and affection. Left unchecked the emotional and energetic disconnect between the couple will grow into a chasm that will be difficult to bridge and return to the place of warmth and affection.

This indicator of a backing off from the emotional connection and commitment to a relationship was captured well in the lyrics of the song, You've Lost That Lovin' Feelin' by the Righteous Brothers.

"You never close your eyes anymore when I kiss your lips

And there's no tenderness like before in your fingertips

You're trying hard not to show it

But baby, baby I know it."

As Jamie Comstock of Butler University aptly pointed out, "You can say, 'I love you' thirty times a day, but if you only touch the person minimally -- rarely hug, kiss, or show appropriate physical affection -- that 'I love you' will ring pretty hollow..."

Ways to Improve:

Make a commitment to give a love touch to your companion every time you are in the same room together. It doesn't need to be a long touch to convey your special level of love to the relationship and bring a smile of delight to your beloved's face and a glowing warmth to their heart. If both of you are committed to improving and nurturing your relationship the love touch you give out will come back to you with equal affection and serenity.

True love is not being with someone because you think you can be happy with that person, but because without that person you know you can never be.

~Unknown

Years from now I can picture us still laughing together, still holding hands, and still completely in love... just like we are now.

Unknown

Last night I looked up at the stars and matched each one with a reason why I love you. I was doing great until I ran out of stars.

~Kelsi

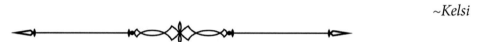

Chapter 11

HOW TO FIND YOUR SOUL MATE EVEN IF YOU CAN'T SEE OR FEEL AURAS

Finding your Soul Mate without the invaluable assistance of being able to see or feel auric fields is certainly more of a challenge. But it is possible. I would still recommend doing the candle exercise outlined in chapter 9 to try to determine some information about who and where your Soul Mate might be. Even if you are drawing a blank with auric abilities you likely have some latent psychic abilities that could still influence the candle flame and provide you with some valuable information.

And there is still much you can do with honest assessment and simple deductive reasoning.

Make a Soul Mate Wish List

There is an old quote that has great truth: "A goal not written is only a wish." Writing your goals, hopes and aspirations down, activates and empowers the energies associated with those goals. Writing down what you seek coalesces and amplifies the energies both within you and without to manifest your desires.

As you contemplate your Soul Mate, make a list writing down every aspect of your ideal mate you can think of. This should include big things like "they are on the same spiritual path" as you are, to small things like "they groom their fingernails nicely." Whatever is important to you in a life mate, big or small, should be on the list. It can include physical aspects about the individual such as "they are physically fit," or "they have long hair," to items about their interests such as "they are a fan of Star Wars." The list itself should have at least twenty-five items to insure you are filling in the picture of your Soul Mate with some completeness. And it can have many more.

The longer your list is the less likely you will be to find someone that meets *all* of the criteria you set forth. But that's OK, realistically, nobody is 100% *perfect* in every aspect. Anyone who meets over 70% of your criteria should be considered a prospective Soul Mate and push you on to the next step in the evaluation.

Even if you neither see nor feel the auric field or the energy centers of the body, you can still use them coupled with your honest mental assessment to make accurate determinations of Soul Mate compatibility.

After someone has passed the first test, meeting at least 70% of the criteria on your Soul Mate Wish List, make an assessment of how compatible you are on each of your seven primary energy centers, plus some conglomerate assessments such as personality.

Xe: How in tune are you psychically? Do you have the same beliefs about psychic powers and abilities? Do you have the same level of desire about exploring and developing your psychic abilities?

Ka: How similar are you in your educational backgrounds and knowledge of the world and various subjects? Surprisingly, many couples can barely talk to each other about anything other than the simplest and mundane of subjects because one has a far less knowledge base and life experience than the other. Soul Mates will always be comparable in this area though their areas of focus may be completely different. Perhaps one studied medicine and the other sociology. But they will both have a comparable level of education and exposure to the world. A good example of a relationship that would be very unlikely to be a Soul Mate, is where one person is a college graduate who has traveled the world somewhat, and the other barely graduated high school and couldn't tell you which continent most countries were on if you named them. This type of Ka disparity could still be Twin Flames, but not Soul Mates.

Qo: This is an often overlooked yet very important area for a successful relationship. The Qo is the well of self-esteem and self-confidence. It doesn't matter whether a prospective Soul Mate is strong or weak in this area. It only matters that they are similar in their level of self-esteem and self-confidence. In relationships where the energy of the Qo is unequal between the two people, it will always result in one partner being domineering in words, actions or attitude over the other, which in turn generates a level of disrespect even if it is not openly expressed. It also creates a relationship dynamic where the less confident and lower self-esteem partner is continually just going along with what their companion prefers or wants to do, rather than having an equal relationship where decisions are jointly made after respectful consideration of both people's opinions.

Ja: the heart center is of course an energy at the forefront of any successful, long-term relationship. Remember, the feelings of passion may not feel as intense with a Soul Mate as they are with a non-Soul Mate (unless you focus on that energy center and will it to be different) because the total of your auric energy is divided over seven energy centers, not concentrated solely in one or two. Like the other energy centers, the important aspect is that both of you are near the same level of passion and feelings of love in your hearts for one another. This includes being on similar levels for your ability to express your affections. If one person loves to cuddle and the other was raised to be more distant and less expressive physically that will likely be an ongoing energy blockage in the relationship. Similarly, if one person easily expresses their love and affection with words, but the other has trouble saying "I love you" because of their personality or upbringing, it will be an ever widening gap in the relationship energy.

Za: This is a rather mysterious energy center to most people. It contains the energies of past-life or pre-existent experiences and primordial fears. Interestingly, the past life experiences do not need to be your own. Though few are aware of this aspect, it is common for people to tune in to past life experiences of others from whom they would derive benefit from their life experiences. This accounts for why so many people think they were Cleopatra or some other famous person in a past life. They were not. But the energetic connection they establish to the real person's memories and experiences is so vivid that they think it was their own life.

When looking for a Soul Mate connection with the Za, the couple should have similar beliefs regarding reincarnation and the afterlife. It doesn't matter whether they believe in reincarnation or disbelieve; just that they are in agreement on what they believe.

With primordial fears such as fear of heights, the more a couple is in sync with their fears or lack of fears, the better. Otherwise situations could arise where one person wants to go forward with an action and the other does not based solely upon their innate fear that the other person has taught themselves to ignore. Just another potential schism driving a wedge in the energy of a relationship.

Wz: This energy center is all about the physical. How strongly a couple is physically attracted to one another projects from the Wz. Ideally both individuals should have a comparable level of physical attraction for one another. Remember, it is not uncommon for the physical attraction between Soul Mates to be less than in common relationships because the auric energy is divided over seven energy centers. The Wz is also responsible for all things pertaining to health and athleticism. Again, look for commonality in these areas. For instance, if one person is a bookworm and the other a fitness nut, that is an incongruent energy that will likely preclude a Soul Mate relationship.

Vm: The energy center of the Vm generates energy of both a creative and sexual nature. Strong sexual attraction for someone issues from the Vm. But so too does a love for art, both as an artist or a connoisseur. This is a very important area to get in sync in a relationship, especially one that is a lifetime Soul Mate union. For example, if one partner is fairly disinterested in sex and the other feels neglected if they don't have sexual relations every day, the energy is in place from the very beginning of a relationship for major problems in the years to come. In regards to a satisfying sex life there's an apropos old saying, "if you have a Ferrari at home you don't care about VW Bugs on the street." Meaning if you have a satisfying sex life with your husband or wife, you will not be looking outside of your marriage for fulfillment.

The creative/artistic side of the Vm needs to also be assessed for compatibility. Art can be a true passion, whether it is art someone is creating or simply an appreciation of a certain type of art. This can express itself in creative hobbies or even professions, or in a passion for collecting, such as coin or antique collecting. Whatever form it manifests itself in, if the creative aspect of the Vm is active it can be quite consuming of a person's free time. Obviously, if it is a passion shared with your partner, it is time invested enriching your relationship with shared experiences. But if one partner has a creative passion and the other is disinterested, the incongruent energy will push people apart over time.

It is not uncommon for both people to have creative interests and expressions that are not the same as their partners. This is not quite as relationship strengthening as having similar creative passions, but it still creates a positive energy bond in a relationship. The key is a similar level of creative passion. Even if it is for different artistic pursuits; perhaps one makes jewelry and the other quilts. Because the level is the same there will be a mutual support, encouragement and understanding of the time and interest committed to the passion for art. There will be an artistic resonance in the couple that is continually thankful for their partners creative, artistic nature.

Personality, Attitude and Appearance

While looking for common energy connections and life experience resonance, it is important to also give weighted consideration to how much you actually enjoy the persons personality and attitude, as well as the ultimate deal maker -- that you enjoy looking at them.

Personality and attitude often work together. Beyond harmony, a prospective life mate and certainly a Soul Mate, should have a personality that simply gives you boundless pleasure to be around, and to hear them talk and laugh. Looks will likely diminish with age, but a great personality in your mate will lighten your life all of your days. Do they exhibit as little or as much spontaneity as you like? Do they make you laugh? Are they romantic enough? Do they remember the little things that mean so much to you? Do they stand by their bedrock principles come hell or high water, including being a reliable rock you can always count on to stand by and support you?

Though attitude can be an intricate part of personality, it can also be separated and should be as you consider if your attitude meshes with your prospective Soul Mates. For instance, perhaps the prospect is into conspiracy theories and thinks the government is secretly out to get them and everybody else in one way or the other. Their attitude is the government is the bad guy. If yours is just the opposite, if you think the government is like a benevolent guardian, those conflicting attitudes and beliefs will herald frictions in the relationship down the road.

One attitude schism I have seen quite often in relationships is how people feel about personal responsibility. Some people always seem to blame everything bad in their life upon something someone else did: their sibling, their boss, their teacher, their parent, the government, anyone but the face they look at in the mirror. Other people are very conscientious about taking at least some responsibility for the bad things that happen in their lives as well as credit for the good. Those two opposing personalities and attitudes would not last long in a fulfilling relationship even if they had many other likes and dislikes in common.

Common Bonds

Distilling it all down to its simplest form, finding your Soul Mate without using energy is all about finding as many common bonds as you can with a person who has a personality that you love and a physical appearance that appeals to your eyes. Even for people who can see or feel auras, it is wise to look at these same connections and qualities from the perspective of everyday life to make an additional assessment of compatibility.

Marriage is not a new institution; it has been around for generations upon generations. There is quite a track record to study to gain an understanding of what factors create a successful lifetime union that is continually expansive and fulfilling for both partners. The one factor that shines through the centuries is the more common interests, goals, mutually respectful and loveable personalities and attitudes each person has, the more likely a blissful, expansive and contented relationship will happily endure through time.

True love is not how you forgive, but how you forget, not what you see but what you feel, not how you listen but how you understand, and not how you let go but how you hold on.

~Unknown

You are my best friend, my shoulder to lean on, the one person I know I can count on, you're the love of my life, you're my one and only, you're my everything.

~Unknown

True love does not keep a record of wrongs. It doesn't need to be perfect. It only needs to be true.

Unknown

Chapter 12

HOW TO NURTURE YOUR LOVE
FOR HAPPILY EVER AFTER

Once you have found your Soul Mate, or the Twin Flame of your choice, you must do more than just rely on your energy connections to see you through your journey together. It will only last a lifetime if it is a priority for both of you and is lovingly nourished every day of your lives. Here are some helpful tips winnowed from the wisdom of many Soul Mate couples whose love and bonds continue to grow stronger and more fulfilling every year of their lives together.

1. Never stop courting

It is easy to let the luster and excitement of a new relationship fade as the mundane routines of life bear down upon you. However, long-term successful love mates never seem to get out of the courtship mode. It may tone down a bit once the relationship is committed. But both partners still remember to regularly do things big and small to present themselves in the best light and let their mate know by word and deed how much they are loved and appreciated.

2. Consciously set aside quality time together every day

This becomes especially important once you have children and pets. Their needs for your time, plus work and what may seem to be an ever expanding list of chores at home, may leave little quality moments for one another in a day. Don't let it be so!

Find a time that works best for the two of you to have some quality alone time even if it is just to talk each day. Maybe in the morning when you awaken, before the daily rush begins, even it means awakening a little earlier to insure time for each other. Evenings before retiring are also a possibility. However, by the end of a long day it is not uncommon for both to no longer be energetic enough for quality time, especially when fatigue is calling you to just lay down and sleep. For some couples the best time is soon after they both get home from work. They make a point of creating quiet moments together, to share a cup of wine or tea, to forget the daily grind in the peace of their home, in the arms of the man or woman they love.

3. Understand and be OK with the fact that there will be bumps in the road

Things can almost seem perfect in any new relationship. That is especially true for Soul Mates or Twin Flames. But real life is not a fairy tale. Even in the very best relationships, the stresses of life get in the way. How a couple deals with financial or health challenges, relationship issues between themselves or in their extended family, work stress and busy life hectic schedules, will go a long way to determining the long-term fulfilling viability of their relationship.

Successful couples understand and accept the reality that after every stressful challenge has passed, there will be another one to take its place at some point in the days to come. They are committed to giving each other 100% support and peacefully and respectfully working out any differences that arise between them while presenting a united front to any forces or people that would harm either one of them or their relationship.

Rich or poor, we all have challenges and though there may be some peaceful respites, eventually new stresses arise and have to be dealt with. The interesting thing about relationship stresses is they will break weak relationships, but will make strong relationships stronger. An apropos relationship slant on an old adage says, "Life is a grindstone. Whether it grinds your relationship down, or polishes it up, depends upon what it is made of."

4. Be committed to your commitment

One of the traits that helps successful life mates weather the storms of life, is if they are willing to make the highest commitment to their partner, usually in the form of marriage and a vow of fidelity. Thus joined, they become determined not to abandon the ship of their relationship no matter how bad the storms of life may swirl. They realize that all storms pass and remaining with their ship is safer and will bring them greater fulfillment and prospects in the future than jumping alone into a tiny lifeboat and leaping into the fury of the storm, hoping for the best.

Of course, there are times when one of the partners may do an act so grievous that it scuttles the relationship ship. It blasts a hole so big in its hull that it can no longer remain afloat. That's a different situation, one that hopefully never arises with Soul Mates or Twin Flames. For any lesser challenge, "united we stand, divided we fall," remains a bedrock truth.

5. Don't scuttle your ship of love by acting like an idiot

What are those idiotic type of actions that blow holes so big your ship will sink regardless of the love or commitment of your partner? Adultery, child abuse, alcoholism, drug addiction and criminal activity of any sort, all demonstrate complete disdain for your partner and your children if you have any. They are usually bombs that blast holes that cannot be repaired, so don't do them.

6. Date night to stay right

An exceptionally helpful part of continuing the courtship process is to make a faithful concerted effort to go on a date with your beloved once every week. It may just be an hour walking through the park, holding hands and talking. But it is also a great time to bring romance back that may be missing during the hurried day cluttered with other people and tasks. This is one-on-one time to share embraces, hugs, kisses, adventures, explorations and rekindling the fires of love, away from any and all everyday distractions from kids, to work or chores.

Though once a week is ideal, your daily life may only allow once or twice a month. Make it something you can both count on and look forward to. Mark it on the calendar. Arrange for a babysitter. If you can't afford a babysitter, do a babysitting swap with friends. One way or another, make it happen regularly and you will reap the rewards of a closer, more fulfilling relationship every day.

7. Forgive and forget, after responsibility accepted

Even in the best of relationships there will be times when your partner does something that justifiably makes you really upset. Not something as big as being unfaithful, but big enough that you can't help wanting to yell at them.

If they were truly responsible for something that angered or hurt you, they need to love you enough to admit their mistake, ask for your forgiveness and do what they can to make amends.

If they do that, you need to forgive them unconditionally, thank them for taking responsibility for their mistake and repairing it as well as they can. Then you need to completely forget that it ever happened and show appreciation and love to your mate.

And truly, to react with calm and acknowledgment of an error is the action of a person far more enlightened than most. The natural reaction when someone starts expressing anger is to yell back at them in defense, even when you are in the wrong. If your partner is better than that and works to fix their mistake, make sure you discard the anger and give them love and appreciation for their efforts.

8. Don't be a simmering pot

Sometimes in "for the relationship," or "for the children," one partner will suffer in silence or near silence while their mate says or does things that bother, offend or even hurt them. This is not a path that helps the relationship or the children. Instead it often leads to a messy relationship end even though it may take some years down the road for it to occur.

Good communication is just as essential for Soul Mates and Twin Flames as it is for anyone else in a romantic, life relationship. It is wise to establish the habit right at the beginning of a relationship that encourages each person to let the other know if anything being said or done is affecting them negatively in any way. Two people in love will have a priority to do whatever they can to bring happiness to the other. If the opposite is occurring, even unknowingly, as is often the case, talking about it early on washes away the energy blockage that was building before it has time to do any damage.

9. Two kisses a day keeps the divorce lawyer away

Of course it is not quite that easy. But small, tokens of affection, especially physical ones, given regularly when you are with each other, such as a kiss in the morning before you part ways for the day and a kiss at night before you close your eyes for sleep, give daily reinforcement to your relationship. Soft touches, eye contact, embraces and kisses affirm, "I love you, appreciate you, and am so thankful you are in my life!"

10. Look for things to praise

Giving praise to others, even someone you love deeply, doesn't come naturally to everyone. Sometimes personality or upbringing conspire to simply not think about it, or even withhold praise. If this is the case, it is a bad habit worth giving concerted effort to break, because sincere praise given with love, is a fresh, uplifting breeze that puts a buoyant wind of happiness into the sails of anyone's ship of life.

Og Mandino in his book *The Greatest Salesman in the World*, pointed out that we are all slaves to our habits. But within that truth, we can choose to be a slave to good habits, such as giving praise easily and frequently, rather than the bad habit of withholding it or making it conditional. Og also pointed out that you can't simply stop the bad habit. You can only get rid of bad habits by replacing them with good habits. In this case, replacing withholding praise with looking for things big and small to regularly compliment your partner and show gratitude and appreciation for. And there are overt praises that are obvious kudos, and covert praises that though more subtle still send a strong message of appreciation. Remember to only give *sincere* compliments. Words that can seem corny when you read them, become endearing and relationship strengthening when spoken with love and sincerity to your beloved.

Need some ideas?

"I thank my lucky stars every day that I married you."

"You handled that situation to perfection."

"You are such a great father/mother. I'm so glad you are the father/mother of our children."

"I love the way you did your hair today."

"That was very ingenious of you."

"You did a great job on that project."

"That outfit looks really good on you."

"I love the way you smile."

"You're amazing. I'm so proud of you."

"I love you so much. How did I ever get so lucky?"

"Thanks for helping with that. It was so much easier with you."

"Wow! You did all that today!"

"Thanks for taking care of that chore."

"You are so smart."

"You have beautiful eyes. I love looking at them."

"Your smile melts my heart as much today as the first day we met."

"You are more attractive to me than any of the stars in the movies."

"Being away from you is hard. I miss you."

"You are my best friend. I'd rather spend time with you than anyone else."

"You have really excellent taste."

"You are perfect for me just the way you are."

"I'm so proud of you."

"You are really good dealing with people."

"I really admire the way you can forgive and forget and not hold grudges."

"Being with you just feels so comfortable."

"You're incredible!"

"Wow! You are looking better and better every day!"

"You're a genius!"

"Wow! Your dinner was like eating at a gourmet restaurant."

"I love it when you do that."

"You are so graceful when you move/walk/dance/run."

"I could really use your advice on this."

"Your cool head got us through that."

"Thanks for being such a hard worker who always does more than their share."

"You have a genuine interest in others that really comes through. It's very admirable."

"You are so sexy."

"Your candor and honesty are very appreciated."

"Can you give me your perspective on this?"

"Sorry if I'm staring. You are like a beautiful piece of art, I just can't take my eyes off of you."

"The greatest blessing God ever gave me is you."

"It's amazing how many guys/girls check you out as you walk by."

"You give the best neck rubs."

"I really respect you for _____."

"You are so funny sometimes. I love that about you."

"I love hearing your voice and talking to you."

"Wow! You make those clothes look good."

"My friends are always telling me how lucky I am to have you."

"My life is complete because you are in it."

"I never imagined a love as wonderful as yours for me and mine for you."

"You inspire me to be the best I can be."

11. "When you have praise, shout it from the rooftop. When you have criticism, bite your tongue."

That was a saying I heard both my mother and father remind me of regularly as I was growing up. It holds especially true for couples that are seeking a long-term, fulfilling relationship and is an integral aspect of Soul Mate and Twin Flame relationships. Praising your spouse, letting them know you recognize and appreciate their excellence and efforts, especially in front of other people, is a small action that brings bountiful rewards. Criticizing your spouse, especially in front of other people, has exactly the opposite effect.

Sometimes criticism just can't be held back. Even in those situations, *learn the distinction between constructive and destructive criticism* and practice giving positive criticism in a loving way. The difference is:

a) the **words you say,**

b) your **tone of voice and manner of speaking** when you say them,

c) and **what words proceeded the criticism**.

Make an extra effort to proceed any criticism with praise, and appreciation creates an entirely different result.

Which of these examples would you respond to more favorably?

"How many times do I have to tell you to put the dishes in the dishwasher? I have asked you to do this a hundred times. Why do you never listen? What is so difficult about rinsing a dish and putting it in the dishwasher? It takes all of ten seconds. You're making more work for me and I'm tired of being your maid."

OR

"Honey, I love you so much for all that you do. And I know after you get home from work you're tired and just want to put off doing anything extra until another time. I feel that way when I come home from a hard day at work too. But neither of us look forward to having to deal with a pile of dirty dishes in the sink. I know we have spoken about this before and I don't want to be a nag, but this is something that is important to me. I really would appreciate it if you would just take an extra ten seconds to rinse your dirty dishes and put them in the dishwasher. Can you please do that for me?"

With the exception of the few unusual people that enjoy arguing, everyone else would surely choose the latter message delivery over the former.

The first message would seem like an attack. The second, like a friendly, loving, respectful request. It will have a lot better reception and likelihood of having the task done as requested.

When attacked with criticism, either harshly or in some cases subtly, it can emotionally throw people back to their childhood when they were scolded by parents, teachers or other adults. This engenders feelings of anger, inadequacy, sadness, vulnerability and fear of consequences.

Criticism also produces one of three distinct reactions

a) Counter-attack

If you are being yelled at -- yell louder. Get bug-eyed, red in the face and make yourself so scary that you cower your opponent and become impervious to their attack. (I work my tail off you SOB!) If you are being accused of inadequacy, hurl the other person even bigger faults back in their face. (Like how many times have I told you to close the toilet seat! And what about that giant mess you just left in the bathroom? Is that something else you just expect me to take care of? You're the one that never listens and doesn't do enough to help out!)

Counter attacks are 100% counter-productive. It turns love partners into adversaries, both trying to win a battle that instead both will lose.

b) Run Away

Many people are greatly traumatized by conflict. When someone starts dumping on them with criticism, especially if it is angry criticism, their reaction is to flee the scene, which for the moment helps remove them emotionally, so they don't feel guilt, afraid, upset, put-downed or wronged. I've actually seen people cover their ears and run away. If the other person is exploding in violent anger, leaving the scene may be the safest and wisest choice at the moment. But it cannot be the standard reaction to criticism. Avoiding the issue just frustrates the other person further and does not make the issue go away. It just makes it simmer. The issue will come up again and because of the continuing unresolved simmer, the explosion will likely be even bigger than before. Loving couples whose relationship is important to them, know that clear, respectful communication is an essential block in the foundation of relationship happiness and longevity.

c) Acquiesce

Sometimes you can give too much trying to please your partner. When one partner is criticizing the other and the person being criticized quickly acquiesces with, "you're right and I'm wrong," they may be setting themselves up for even more criticism in the future because dominating them was so easy. More often than not, when this is said it isn't because the person actually feels they were being justifiably criticized, but simply because they don't want to continue in an argument. A festering resentment of their spouse is usually the end result.

Couples with strong bonds learn how to work through frictions with love and mutual respect by listening sincerely to the other person, speaking softly not harshly, and responding with praise as well as critique or complaint.

Don't think you are being helpful by being critical

The first question to ask yourself before you say anything critical is, "Is this something I need to say?" Unsolicited critique or criticism, when someone didn't ask for your opinion, is seldom desired and almost never appreciated.

Some people develop a bad habit to critique or criticize others, justifying their actions by thinking they are actually helping them by pointing out their faults or shortcomings. However, most people are very aware of their faults and shortcomings and don't need anyone to point them out, unless they have specifically asked for their opinion and constructive criticism. For instance, telling your friend, spouse or family member that they should probably lose weight for the sake of their health is a subtle criticism, even though it may be true. It is not something they are not already aware of. By pointing it out you are simply reminding them that they are overweight and making them feel undesirable.

12. Don't keep score

A sure way to always find your relationship lacking is to keep a mental score about how much you are doing compared to how much your partner is doing. This will continually frame your relationship in negativity. It can run the gamut from who contributes more financially, to who does more chores, to who expresses love to a greater extent, to who is more responsible, to who does more to maintain family unity and harmony and on and on and on. If you want your relationship to last and thrive you simply cannot do this – at all!

In a healthy relationship with reciprocity, there will be no basis for keeping score. Both partners will always be motivated from love and devotions to do all they can, each in their own way, to contribute to the health and happiness of the relationship and family. And each person will recognize, appreciate and acknowledge the efforts of their partner.

If you are in a relationship where it is difficult not to keep score because there is such a yawning gap between your efforts and work compared to your partner's contributions, the inequality points to deeper problems. If you work a job then come home tired, to piles of chores, while your partner sits around, drinking beer, watching TV, wondering when dinner will be ready and the laundry done -- sadly, that usually stems from a lifetime of bad habits that are very unlikely to change especially if they didn't change at the inception of the relationship, the time your partner wanted to please you the most. In those cases, love yourself enough to not be a martyr. You deserve better and better is out there waiting for you.

In seeking your Soul Mate or Twin Flame you will find a person who is always seeking ways to make your relationship better and more fulfilling for you. They derive great joy from seeing you happy. As both people see their life together through the same window of the others happiness, both naturally end up doing all they can to make it so.

13. Dedicate the first year to each other

This is not as necessary for couples who have closely known each other for years. But for everyone else, an exceptionally valuable block in the relationship foundation is laid down when a couple dedicates their first year of married life to spending as much time as possible with each other. Lifetime habits of love, understanding, devotion and desire to bring a smile and happiness to the other are created within this cocoon of special time together.

If possible, avoid stress inducers and time gulpers such as: an intense college curriculum, a high-pressure hour-eating job, starting a new business, and even pregnancy. Create as much time for each other and as little time for everyone and everything else, and you will forge an amazing bond and be remembering and thanking yourselves for making that choice every year of your lives together.

14. Couples that play together stay together

Having active entertainment and recreation interests that you can enjoy together with fun and laughter, without getting riled up in competitive activities, is a particularly valuable couples bonding tool.

Though each person will likely still have hobbies, entertainment and recreation choices that their partner has little interest in, frequently sharing ones they do both enjoy is a love unifier. It can be anything from playing cards or board games, to hikes, to racket sports, or concerts where they appreciate the same music. The two main ingredients are a level of active participation and that it is something special, not an everyday occurrence. For those reasons it does not include passively sitting together watching television shows, which creates little or no interaction and is sufficiently mind-numbing in that many people cannot even remember the plot of shows they watched the previous night.

Though they are less passive than hiking or racket sports, concerts and theater movies or plays are still dynamic joint entertainment because they are set apart as special dates, with specific shared pleasure in the entertainment. Plus, as set aside dates a concert, theater movie or play will likely be enjoyed sitting closely side-by-side, holding hands and proceeded or followed by a romantic dinner date.

15. Spice life with spontaneity and surprise

This goes well with remembering the little things. Some people claim they don't like spontaneity or surprise and that's fine. That truly is some peoples personality – up to a point. What they usually really mean is they don't like having their planned schedule disrupted. This trait tends to get more pronounced as people age. No problem, just work your surprise or planned spontaneity into their schedule. Let them know they need to block out certain hours for a surprise you have planned. That little trick will insure they are looking forward with curiosity to the surprise rather than being upset with having their schedule disrupted. Even spontaneity can be planned. Again, just ask them to block out some time for you on a day when you both have no other plans. Once your time arrives, start thinking about what you are going to do -- totally spontaneous within a planned time frame!

16. Remember the little things – everyday.

The occasional big presents and tokens of loving sentiment are nice, but it is the everyday little acts of affection and appreciation that count the most. A momentary loving touch; a warm smile; a sweet endearment whispered unexpectedly in the ear; doing your part for chores around the house; a surprise hug from behind; a long, loving gaze; reaching out and holding hands while walking; always speaking respectfully; surprise cleaning and washing of their car; a hand placed softly on your partners thigh while you sit, remembering to say thank you and show gratitude; these are among the little jewels of love, worth more than gold.

In addition to soft touches and unexpected expressions of love and appreciation, here are some ideas for little things that mean a lot! Most of them have the greatest impact if they are done unexpectedly and not for a usual special occasion like a birthday, anniversary or Valentine's Day.

a) ***Give your lover a foot rub when you are sitting together*** on the couch watching a show. Inevitably it will turn into a mutual foot rub, so you get as much as you give!

b) ***Leave short written notes in surprising places.*** "I love you!" "You're the greatest!" "You're my dream come true!" "I can't believe how lucky I am to have you as my wife/husband." "I'll have something special for you when you get home tonight." Place your notes in locations you know they will find them as a surprise during the day. Some good spots include, inside their eye glasses case, on the steering wheel of their car, inside a cabinet they open every day, on their hand mirror, on their shaving razor, in their coat pocket, replacing the bookmark in the book they are reading, inside their lunch bag, an email on their computer, or a screen saver!

c) Say thank you. Simply giving sincere thanks, especially for small efforts, is quite a warming balm to the heart and increases the bonds of love.

d) ***Mail a card of love for no occasion.*** Don't wait for a birthday, anniversary or Valentine's Day. Send him/her a special card where you personally write about your affections and appreciation. Because it isn't for a particular occasion it may mean much more. You are expected to think of your loved one on regular holidays. When you show you are thinking about them on other days, it is a testimony to the depth of your affection.

e) ***Send her/him a card or email with something funny.*** This is especially effective if you can relate it to something funny the two of you experienced together. People remember times they laughed together about something they were experiencing. For example, a card with a picture of a small dock going out into a placid lake. Hand written inside, "This reminded me of the time I jumped in the lake and pulled you in with me."

f) Compliment them about the way they look, their clothes, how they smell, the way their new hair cut makes them look younger or more beautiful or virile.

g) ***Make them breakfast in bed.*** Always a great romantic way to show you love and appreciate your spouse. It works best when it is done spontaneously and not for a particular occasion.

h) ***Do a task they hate for them*** and let it be a surprise discovery. When someone is dreading doing a chore they have to do and then to their delight discover their lover has done it for them, it lights a lot of fires of love.

i) ***Lighten their mood with music.*** On a day when you get home before your companion, put on their favorite music. Their mood and thoughts of you will be buoyed from the moment they cross the threshold. Music, if it is a type that a person resonates with, touches their soul. If you are the one that made it possible, so do you.

j) ***Watch the video or look at the pictures of your marriage and early years together.*** Often times a walk down memory lane reminds both of you of why you got together in the first place and brings up happy memories from the past. Looking back on all the good times you've shared is a reminder of how special your relationship is; something that can sometimes be forgotten in the hustle and bustle and challenges of life.

k) ***Do it- finally!*** There is always something your spouse has asked you to do that you have neglected taking care of: someone to call, an appointment needing to be set; taking a pile of old clothes to the second hand store; cleaning out the closet or the shed.

l) ***The reverse neck kiss & hug.*** Guaranteed to let him or her know you love and appreciate them without saying a word! Without scaring them, come up behind your companion, put your arms around their waist and nuzzle their neck, then kiss them softly in multiple places along their neck and behind the erogenous zone of their ear. It will be a sign of affection they will not ignore, but will turn and reciprocate with a warm heart. If you are a short woman and want to do this with your man, wait until they are seated in a chair you can easily come up behind.

m) ***Text or sext your lover messages throughout the day.*** From innocent thoughts of affection like, "I'm thinking of you and your big blue eyes," to erotic pictures or texts. Send them something every hour and they may need to come home early in their excitement to be with you.

n) ***Spontaneously go out to eat*** on a night when one or both of you come home tired from work. If neither has to cook or clean up the kitchen, a task that was probably being dreaded, it makes the tiring day be almost completely forgotten. As an extra love boost, when the situation arises and your companion doesn't like the meal they ordered, switch plates with them and give them yours or share both together.

o) Offer to help. Each person typically gets into the habit of doing certain chores -- his chores and her chores. Unexpectedly coming and helping your companion with chores they were expecting to have to do on their own, will always bring a smile of appreciation and sometime much more!

p) ***Give a foot bath and rub.*** Let them sit back and watch their favorite movie or show while you stick their tired bare feet in a basin of hot (but not too hot) water with Epsom Salts you've prepared. After the water begins to cool give them a foot massage to finish off the surprise.

q). ***Give them a candle-lit bath and towel rub.*** Prepare a warm bath for them and light the room with candles or LED candles, put on their favorite music and scent the water with their favorite essential oil. When they come out give them a vigorous towel rub over every part of their body to dry them off.

r) ***Make a secret pampering appointment for them***, but not for a special occasion. Find something you know they will really love like a professional massage or a manicure. Tell them you have a surprise for them and that they need to set aside a certain time. Pick them up and let it be a surprise where you are taking them.

s) ***Slave for a day.*** This can be real fun for both of you. The basic premise is to simply serve and pamper them in every way. Make all their meals, bring them their drinks, open doors for them, prepare their bath, if they want something you get up and get it. If you want to carry the theme into the bedroom, it can add quite the spice to intimacy.

t) ***Public kiss is a can't miss.*** Showing your affection with a kiss in public, the more people that see it the better, shows your companion you are proud to love them and not bashful to let everyone know.

u) ***Play games together.*** Great for a rainy weekend day. Get out your favorite board games, card games, or Ninetendo Wii game. Relax and have fun together without getting too competitive. Later in the evening there might be some bedroom games you prefer over parlor games.

v) ***Lover's nickname and terms of endearment.*** Having someone you love call you by a pet name just makes you feel special. The name itself seems unimportant. In France, I've heard people call their lover "mon grand can" (my big duck) and "mon petit chou" (my little cabbage). In America I've heard people call their companion "peanut," "burp" "bear" and "old shoe." Those interesting terms of endearment seem to melt hearts and bring smiles despite the less than flattering terms. So the effect is obviously in appreciation for having a special nickname or endearment and not necessarily in what the words are actually depicting. Similarly, terms of endearment like "honey," "sweetie," "darl'in," "sweetheart," "love," "lover," and "babe," should be used often in place of their given name, setting you and your affections for them apart and above everyone else.

w) ***Hold hands, sit close, never lose your young love.*** Touch is an incredible conveyer of love and affection. If you've ever looked at old married couples, those that have been together for more than three decades, you'll occasionally see couples who act like they are still newlyweds. They always sit next to each other, still walk down the street holding hands, and when you see them look into each other's eyes you can't hope but notice the sparkling look of love they share with each other. Being able to express their love so fully after so many years, didn't just happen to them. You know it is something they have worked at and made a priority for all of their lives together. A good lesson for all of us.

x) ***Run your fingers through their hair*** and gently run your fingernails over their scalp for a few minutes just as they lay down to go to sleep. This is incredibly relaxing and warmly endearing and appreciated.

y) ***Late night treats.*** Make an excuse to go to the store for something a couple of hours before bed and come home with your lovers favorite dessert.

z) Don't be hesitant to say "I'm sorry," when it is appropriate. Being willing to admit fault when you have truly made an error is a distinction of a higher being and a trait of strong couples.

All relationships take dedication and effort to help them last through the years and get past life challenges still united. You can't forget to show your love every day in small ways. A love relationship is like the most beautiful of all flowers, with an alluring scent that is intoxicating and a wonder that enraptures. But for it to remain forever in all its glory, like any delicate flower it must be nurtured conscientiously and consistently.

Twin Flames and Soul Mates begin with the advantage of having more harmonious energy connections and common interests and goals than run-of-the-mill relationships. But in that extra boost do not become complacent. All relationships that last, continuing to help each person grow and expand and into the crescendo of their potential and fulfillment of their happiness, do so only because that was the objective from the very first day and the effort made every day of their lives together to make it so.

May you find and love your Soul Mate through all your days of life and beyond. It is the greatest fulfillment you will ever know -- if you make it so.

Namaste,

Embrosewyn

I WISH I COULD GO BACK IN TIME
AND FIND YOU SOONER, THAT
WAY I COULD LOVE YOU LONGER.

~UNKNOWN

You are my life... when you're with me I am speechless... when I see you my knees go weak... if I had a rose for every time I kissed you I would walk through a never ending garden...
I love you.

`*Unknown*

~♥~

ABOUT THE AUTHOR

One of my first childhood memories was of seeing beautiful rainbow auras of light around the heads of people young and old. It began a lifetime of observation, study and experimentation with a wide variety of psychic and paranormal phenomena that has now eclipsed six decades.

Married to my exploration of the supernatural has been a deep spiritual journey to understand and commune with the source of all the magic I found in the world. It has not been merely an intellectual exercise for me. In times more than I can count, I have experienced the wonder and power of the supernatural. Call it magic, magick or miracles, I know they are real, because I have lived and experienced them, time and time again.

I realize my life's journey has been a true blessing greater than I can ever pay back. This has certainly influenced me with a passionate desire to help the people of the world. Many of my books are written with that goal in mind. I believe there is greatness inside every person, calling for someone even greater to emerge. Knowing the secrets to unleashing the magic inside of you is more empowering than anything you can imagine. Your possibilities are as limitless as your imagination, coupled with your knowledge, and your desire to make it so.

I've been fortunate to have traveled to many countries around the world and have interacted with people from the president of the country to the family living in a shack with a dirt floor. Being among people of many cultures, religions and social standings, watching them in their daily lives, seeing their hopes and aspirations for their children and the joys they have with their families and friends, has continually struck me with a deep feeling of oneness. I've been with elderly people as they breathed their last breath and at the birth of babies when they take their first. It's all very humbling. This amazing world we live in and the wonderful people that fill it have given me so much. Writing and sharing the secrets of how everyone can experience magic in their life, is my way to give back as much as I can to as many people as I can.

I may not be your first love, first kiss, first sight, or first date but I just want to be your last

~Unknown

~♥~

EMBROSEWYN'S BOOKS

WORDS OF POWER AND TRANSFORMATION
101+ Magickal Words and Sigils of Celestine Light To Manifest Your Desires

Whatever you seek to achieve or change in your life, big or small, Celestine Light magickal words and sigils can help your sincere desires become reality.

Drawing from an ancient well of magickal power, the same divine source used by acclaimed sorcerers, witches and spiritual masters through the ages, the 101+ magickal words and sigils are revealed to the public for the very first time. They can create quick and often profound improvements in your life.

It doesn't matter what religion you follow or what you believe or do not believe. The magickal words and sigils are like mystical keys that open secret doors regardless of who holds the key. If you put the key in and turn it, the door will open and the magick will swirl around you!

From the beginner to the Adept, the Celestine Light words of power and sigils will expand your world and open up possibilities that may have seemed previously unachievable. Everything from something simple like finding a lost object, to something powerful like repelling a psychic or physical attack, to something of need such as greater income, to something life changing like finding your Soul Mate.

Some may wonder how a few spoken words combined with looking for just a moment at a peculiar image could have such immediate and often profound effects. The secret is these are ancient magick words of compelling power and the sigils are the embodiment of their magickal essence. Speaking or even thinking the words, or looking at or even picturing the sigil in your mind, rapidly draws angelic and magickal energies to you like iron to a magnet to fulfill the worthy purpose you desire.

This is a book of potent white magick of the light. Without a lot of training or ritual, it gives you the ability to overcome darkness threatening you from inside or out. For what is darkness except absence of the light? When light shines, darkness fades and disappears, not with a roar, but with a whimper.

Use the words and sigils to call in the magickal energies to transform and improve your life in every aspect. In this comprehensive book you will find activators to propel your personal growth, help you excel in school, succeed in your own business, or launch you to new heights in your profession. It will give you fast acting keys to improve your relationships, change your luck, revitalize your health, and develop and expand your psychic abilities.

Embrosewyn Tazkuvel is an Adept of the highest order in Celestine Light. After six decades of using magick and teaching it to others he is now sharing some of the secrets of what he knows with you. Knowledge that will instantly connect you to divine and powerful universal forces that with harmonic resonance, will unleash the magickal you!

Inside you will discover:

- 101 word combinations that call in magickal forces like a whirlwind of light.
- 177 magickal words in total.
- 101 sigils to go with each magickal word combination to amplify the magickal results you seek.
- 101 audio files you can listen to; helping you have perfect pronunciation of the Words of Power regardless of your native language. Available directly from the eBook and with a link in the paperback edition.

AURAS
How To See, Feel & Know

TOP REVIEWS

#1 Amazon bestseller in multiple categories since 2012. Used as a comprehensive reference book in aura and chakra classes around the world. Filled with real life accounts of Embrosewyns adventures with auras, plus 47 **full color** pictures and illustrations, with 17 dynamic eye exercises to help you rapidly begin to see the beautiful world of auras.

"Mr. Tazkuvel does a wonderful job at making such a complicated and specific subject like auras easy to learn while entertaining the reader with his own experiences as an aura reader throughout his life. The guide is well-written, casual but informative, vivid with imagery (from pictures to illustrations), provides tips/tools for training the mind/eyes and ensures that the reader gets a comprehensive guide to auras in a real and tangible way." ~**R. Coker, Amazon Top 1000 Reviewer**

"This is one of the most interesting books I have read to date. I had absolutely no idea that I could 'train' myself to see auras! Although I still have a ways to go, I can honestly tell that I am able to pick up on people's auras. The parts on body language and the authors personal story were icing on the cake. Loved it and will definitely be telling everyone I know about it!" ~**Momto4BookLover, Amazon Top 2000 Reviewer**

"I was a huge skeptic and got the book thinking I was going to blast it in the reviews. After reading through it though I realize that I was completely wrong! The author does a great job explaining exactly what an aura is, as well as how to interpret them. There are very good exercises to help you train your eyes to see auras." ~**Irish Times, Amazon Top 2000 Reviewer**

***Auras: How to See, Feel & Know,* is like three books in one!**

- It's an entertaining read as Embrosewyn recalls his early childhood and high school experiences seeing auras, and the often humorous reactions by everyone from his mother to his friends when he told them what he saw.

- It is also a complete training manual to help you quickly be able to see Auras in vibrant color. It includes 17 eye exercises and dozens of Full Color pictures, enabling anyone with vision in both eyes to begin seeing vividly colored auras around any person. The secret is in retraining the focusing parts of your eyes to see things that have always been there, but you have never been able to see before. Auras: How to See, Feel & Know, includes all the power techniques, tools and Full Color eye exercises from Embrosewyn's popular workshops.

- Additionally, there is a fascinating chapter on body language. Embrosewyn teaches in his workshops to not just rely on your interpretation of the aura alone, but to confirm it with another indicator such as body language. Auras: How to See, Feel & Know goes in depth with thorough explanations and great pictures to show you all the common body language indicators used to confirm what someone's aura is showing you.

For those who already have experience seeing auras, the deeper auric layers and subtle auric nuances and the special ways to focus your eyes to see them, are explained in detail, with accompanying Full Color pictures to show you how the deeper layers and auric aberrations appear.

Secret Earth Series

INCEPTION
BOOK 1

TOP REVIEWS

"I simply couldn't put it down! It has, in some ways, changed the very way I think. It's exciting, adventurous and keeps you hanging on to the edge of your seat throughout! You don't wanna miss this one!" ~**Barbara Cary, Amazon Top 1000 Reviewer**

"The writing is clear and vivid, both opening doors in readers' imaginations and making heady concepts accessible at the same time." ~**Alex Prosper, Amazon Top 1000 Reviewer**

"What an adventurous and mind-captivating story! I absolutely loved it! If you are like me, you will find yourself not being able to put this book down until it is finished. That's how good it is. I could easily see it being made into a full-scale Hollywood movie." ~**Anna , Amazon Top 5000 Reviewer**

Could it be possible that there is a man alive on the Earth today that has been here for two thousand years? How has he lived so long? And why? What secrets does he know? Can his knowledge save the

Earth or is it doomed?

Continuing the epic historical saga begun in the *Oracles of Celestine Light*, but written as a novel rather than a chronicle, Inception unveils the life and adventures of Lazarus of Bethany and his powerful and mysterious sister Miriam of Magdala.

The first book of the Secret Earth series, **Inception**, reveals the hidden beginnings of the strange, secret life of Lazarus. From his comfortable position as the master of caravans to Egypt he is swept into a web of intrigue involving his enigmatic sister Miriam and a myriad of challenging dangers that never seem to end and spans both space and time.

Some say Miriam is an angel, while others are vehement that she is a witch. Lazarus learns the improbable truth about his sister, and along with twenty-three other courageous men and women, is endowed with the secrets of immortality. But he learns that living the secrets is not as easy as knowing them. And living them comes at a price; one that needs to be paid in unwavering courage, stained with blood, built with toil, and endured with millenniums of sacrifice, defending the Earth from all the horrors that might have been. Inception is just the beginning of their odyssey.

DESTINY
BOOK 2

In preparation, before beginning their training as immortal Guardians of the Earth, Lazarus of Bethany and his wife Hannah were asked to go on a short visit to a world in another dimension. "Just to look around a bit and get a feel for the differences," Lazarus's mysterious sister, Miriam of Magdala assured them.

She neglected to mention the ravenous monstrous birds, the ferocious fire-breathing dragons, the impossibly perfect people with sinister ulterior motives, and the fact that they would end up being naked almost all the time! And that was just the beginning of the challenges!

LOVE YOURSELF
The Secret Key to Transforming Your Life

TOP REVIEWS

"Great book on loving yourself which is the most important part of love. Packed with wisdom and the videos are fantastic. If you want to get more out of life and be a better person to yourself, to others and the world this is a highly recommended read." **K. Allen   Amazon Top 1000 Reviewer**

"Wow, is all I can say. I read this book in one sitting and I have to say that it was an amazing read. ...what the author has to say will transform your life. The 88 reasons to love were inspirational, I felt my spirit soar as I read each one." **Focusman**

Loving yourself is all about energy. As humans we devote a great deal of our energy through our time, thoughts and emotions to love. We read about it, watch movies and shows about it, dream about it, hope for it to bless our lives, feel like something critically important is lacking when it doesn't, and at the very least keep a sharp eye out for it when its missing.

Too often we look to someone else to fulfill our love and crash and burn when relationships end, or fail to live up to our fantasies of what we thought they should be. Helping those situations to never occur begins with loving yourself first. It is a precious gift from you to you. An incredibly powerful energy that not only enhances your ability to give love more fully to others, but also creates a positive energy of expanding reverberation that brings more love, friendship and appreciation to you from all directions. It is the inner light that illuminates your life empowering you to create the kind of life you desire and dream. Helping you along the way, you'll find a gift inside of 88 reasons to love yourself.

Special Bonus: Love Yourself is ALSO AVAILABLE AS AN AUDIO BOOK! This allows you to listen and read at the same time!

22 STEPS TO THE LIGHT OF YOUR SOUL

TOP REVIEWS

This is a beautiful book. The word "generous" comes to mind. It's presented in such a way that you don't need to retain or absorb a whole lot of information at once - you can just dip into certain parts, and save others for later... so good. It opened my imagination and set my spirit spinning with possibilities and ideas. It's rare to find a book with this effect. The authors writing grabbed me from the get-go; it's charming, smooth, and intelligent without being pretentious. An amazing read. ~**Holly Wood, Amazon Top 4000 Reviewer**

There is something at work when you read the pages of this book. It feels like you are reading a dream. Not a scary dream, yet a dream where you are a little on edge. In this intimate book, the author shares with you his journey and the knowledge he has unlocked. The dream like feeling is maybe your mind awakening. I have read many of these new-age books during the past year. I can tell you that this is more advanced than many. It is challenging if you are new on your journey, yet it is fulfilling. 5/5 stars. ~**G. McFadden, Amazon Top 12,000 Reviewer**

What would it be like if you could reach through space and time to query the accumulated wisdom of the ages and get an answer to the mist vexing questions in your own life? *22 Steps to the Light of Your Soul* reveals such treasured insights, eloquently expounding upon the foundational principles of 22 timeless subjects of universal interest and appeal, to help each reader grow and expand into their fullest potential.

In a thought-provoking, poetic writing style, answers to questions we all ponder upon, such as love, happiness, success and friendship, are explored and illuminated in short, concise chapters, perfect for a thought to ponder through the day or contemplate as your eyes close for sleep.

Each paragraph tells a story and virtually every sentence could stand alone as an inspiring quote on your wall.

22 Steps to the Light of Your Soul is also available as an AUDIO BOOK.

ORACLES OF CELESTINE LIGHT
Complete Trilogy Of Genesis, Nexus And Vivus
TOP REVIEWS

I I have never read a book more touching and enlightening as this Trilogy of books! This book is for anyone searching for truth in whatever form or place it may be found. It will resonate with you to your very soul if have an open mind to see it. This is what I have been searching for, the missing pieces to the puzzle, the mysteries, the deeper teachings of Yeshua. Thank you so much for sharing this treasure with the world, my life is ever enriched because of it! ~**Jamie, Amazon Top 1000 Reviewer**

ts hard to describe, but reading the details of the garden of Eden, to Adam and Eve, to their banishment, was more complete and plausible than anything the bible states. For starters, it wasn't just Adam and Eve, but 12 men and 12 woman, and from them they built up the human race in the garden, and were called Edenites. This is just a small taste of the astounding history that fills in the gaps that the bible has. This book, especially for the very religious, might be hard to read, but I implore you to give it an open mind. You might just find your entire world, and spiritual view, will be opened up. ~**Jamie, Amazon Top 1000 Reviewer**

The controversial Oracles of Celestine Light, is a portal in time to the days of Yeshua of Nazareth, over 2000 years ago, revealed in fulfilling detail to the world by the reclusive Embrosewyn Tazkuvel. It includes 155 chapters of sacred wisdom, miracles and mysteries revealing life-changing knowledge about health, longevity, happiness and spiritual expansion that reverberates into your life today.

Learn the startling, never before understood truth about: aliens, other dimensions, Atlantis, Adam & Eve, the Garden of Eden, Noah and the ark, giants, the empowerment of women, dreams, angels, Yeshua of Nazareth (Jesus), his crucifixion & resurrection, his wife Miriam of Magdala (Mary Magdala), Yudas Iscariot (Judas), the afterlife, reincarnation, energy vortexes, witches, magic, miracles, paranormal abilities, and you!

The Oracles of Celestine Light turns accepted religious history and traditional teachings on their head. But page by page, it makes more sense than anything you´ve ever read and shares simple yet profound truths to make your life better today and help you to understand and unleash your miraculous potential.

The Oracles of Celestine Light explains who you are, why you are here, and your divine destiny. It is a must-read for anyone interested in spirituality, personal growth and thought-provoking answers to the unknown. Unknown

PSYCHIC SELF DEFENSE

TOP REVIEW

Regardless of your beliefs, its an elegantly composed and greatly fascinating book. The writer's composing style easy is to follow through. I've read a couple of pages I ended up unable to put the book down. Assuming that you've generally been fascinated about whether psychic capabilities are "genuine" or perhaps that you have some of your own, this is really the book that you need to peruse. ~**Jayden Sanders, Amazon Top 10,000 Reviewer**

Have you ever felt a negative energy come over you for no apparent reason when you are near someone or around certain places? Psychic Self Defense details 17 common psychic threats, with exact, effective counter measures including many real life examples from Embrosewyn's 5 decades of personal experiences with the paranormal, devising what works and what doesn't from hard won trial and error.

Both the neophyte and the experienced will find a wealth of specific how-to methods to counter all forms of psychic attacks: from projections of negative thoughts from other people, to black magic curses, to hauntings by disembodied spirits, to energy sucking vampires, or attacks by demons.

Psychic Self Defense should be in the library of every psychic and serious student of the paranormal, and absolutely read by every medium, channeler, or person who makes any contact with forces, entities, or beings from the world beyond.

Psychic Self Defense is also available as an AUDIO BOOK.

UNLEASH YOUR PSYCHIC POWERS

TOP REVIEWS

"Along with information on auras, channeling and animal whispering it contains just about every psychic and paranormal topic you can think of. The section on Ki energy was also very good- make that excellent. The author really over delivers in material and it is a nice change from books with hardly any info." ~**Diana L., Amazon Top 500 Reviewer**

"The author shows a skill for weaving words and explaining the intricacies of the wealth of psychic realms, managing to introduce me to all the many psychic areas a person could become proficient in... and then he showed me how to begin my journey of uncovering my own talents in the psychic world. From a reader's standpoint, the book is filled with countless insights into psychic powers/abilities as well as a deeper understanding of how to train your mind/body to become in tune with the psychic world." ~**L. Collins, Amazon Top 1000 Reviewer**

"A welcome relief. I was a little skeptical about the validity of the contents of this book . . . UNTIL I read it. Being a paranormal researcher myself, and up-to-date on psychic phenomena, the ins and outs, the dos and don'ts, and all the scams in-between, I was ready for a none too favorable review. How nice to be disappointed! This impressive book is very well written; and remarkably - it is comprehensive

without being boring. I strongly suggest that you read it from cover to cover BEFORE delving into the supernatural world of Psychic Power - from Channeling to Psychic Self Defense, and Telepathy to my personal favorite- Lucid Dreams." ~**Lyn Murray, Author-Poet Laureate-Artist**

A comprehensive guidebook for all levels of practitioners of the psychic and paranormal arts. Each one of the twenty supernatural abilities presented, including Clairvoyance, Animal Whispering, Lucid Dreaming, Precognition, Astral Projection, Channeling, Telekinesis and Telepathy, include easy-to-follow, step-by-step instructions on how you can unleash the full potential of these potent powers in your own life. Spiced with personal stories of Embrosewyn's five decades of experience discovering, developing and using psychic and paranormal talents. Paranormal abilities have saved Embrosewyn's life and the lives of his family members on multiple occasions. Learning to fully develop your own supernatural talents may come in just as handy one day.

Psychic Awakening Series
CLAIRVOYANCE
BOOK 1

TOP REVIEW

For those who don't know what Clairvoyance is, check this book out and learn. Even if you don't believe it, read it anyway. I learned quite a bit more than I originally knew about it. Check it out! ~**Cayce Hrivnak, Amazon Top 15,000 Reviewer**

Would it be helpful to you if you could gain hidden knowledge about a person, place, thing, event, or concept, not by any of your five physical senses, but with visions and "knowing?" *Clairvoyance* takes you on a quest of self-discovery and empowerment, helping you unlock this potent ability in your life. It includes riveting personal stories from Embrosewyn's six decades of psychic and paranormal adventures, plus fascinating accounts of others as they discovered and cultivated their supernatural abilities.

Clearly written, step-by-step practice exercises will help you to expand and benefit from your own clairvoyant abilities. This can make a HUGE improvement in your relationships, career and creativity. As Embrosewyn has proven from over twenty years helping thousands of students to find and develop their psychic and paranormal abilities, EVERYONE, has one or more supernatural gifts. *Clairvoyance* will help you discover and unleash yours!

TELEKINESIS
BOOK 2

TOP REVIEWS

Telekinesis is a great read. The author is a gifted storyteller and his personal experiences and journey are captivating and give some nice insight into focusing. The best parts of the book are how much time is spent on the different exercises and experiments that are here to help you practice and expand your abilities. ~**D Roberts, Amazon Top 6000 Reviewer**

This author does an excellent job of describing events that have happened to him and others pertaining to telekinesis. He also gives an outstanding explanation of what it actually is and how it works. I believe that anyone that is interested in harnessing this ability should take the time to read this fantastic book and learn from someone who has actually had these experiences himself. ~**L. Harrison, Amazon Top 10,000 Reviewer**

Telekinesis, also known as psychokinesis, is the ability to move or influence the properties of objects without physical contact. Typically it is ascribed as a power of the mind. But as Embrosewyn explains, based upon his 5 decades of personal experience, the actual physical force that moves and influences objects emanates from a person's auric field. It initiates with a mental thought, but the secret to the power is in your aura!

This book is filled with proven, exercises and training techniques to help you unlock this formidable paranormal ability. Spiced with accounts of real-life experiences by both Embrosewyn and others, you'll be entertained while you learn. But along the way you will begin to unleash the potent power of *Telekinesis* in your own life!

DREAMS
BOOK 3

TOP REVIEW

Spellbound with this book. A fantastic and informative read. ~ **Brandy**

In *Dreams*, renowned psychic/paranormal practitioner Embrosewyn Tazkuvel reveals some of his personal experiences with the transformational effect of dreams, while sharing time-tested techniques and insights that will help you unlock the power of your own night travels.

An expanded section on Lucid Dreaming gives you proven methods to induce and expand your innate ability to control your dreams. It explores the astonishing hidden world of your dream state that can reveal higher knowledge, greatly boost your creativity, improve your memory, and help you solve vexing problems of everyday life that previously seemed to have no solution.

Detailing the nine types of dreams will help you to understand which dreams are irrelevant and which you should pay close attention to, especially when they reoccur. You'll gain insight into how to interpret the various types of dreams to understand which are warnings of caution, and which are gems of inspiration that can change your life from the moment you awaken and begin to act upon that which you dreamed.

Dreaming while you sleep is a part of your daily life and cumulatively it accounts for dozens of years of your total life. It is a valuable time of far more than just rest. Become the master of your dreams and your entire life can become more than you ever imagined possible. Your dreams are the secret key to your future.

A Note From Embrosewyn About Your Soul Name

As many people who have read my books or attended my seminars over the years are aware, one of the things I use my psychic gifts for is to discover a person's Soul Name. Knowing this name and the meaning and powers of the sounds has proven to be transformational in the lives of some people. It has always been a great privilege for me to be asked to find a Soul Name for someone. But as my books have become more popular and numerous over the years, with new titles actively in the works in both the *Secret Earth series* and the *Awakening Psychic series*, plus sequels to popular stand alone books such as *Auras*, I have less and less time available to discover a Soul Name for someone when they request it. Doing so requires up to 2 hours of uninterrupted meditation time, which is a fairly great challenge for me to find these days.

With these time constraints in mind, it will generally be five to seven days once I receive your picture before I can get back to you with your Soul Name. I do hope everyone will understand. If you would like to know more about Soul Names please visit this site, *www.mysoulname.com*.

Namaste,

Embrosewyn

Before you go...one last thing

If you have enjoyed *Soul Mate Auras*, I would be honored if you would take a few moments to revisit the book page on Amazon and leave a nice review. Thank you!

47482146R00084

Made in the USA
San Bernardino, CA
06 April 2017